WEB 2.0

Web 2.0 is a highly accessible introductory text examining all the crucial discussions and issues that surround the changing nature of the World Wide Web. It not only contextualizes Web 2.0 within the history of the Web, but also goes on to explore its position within the broader dispositif of emerging media technologies.

The book uncovers the connections between diverse media technologies including mobile smartphones, hand-held multimedia players, "netbooks" and electronic book readers such as the Amazon Kindle, all of which are made possible only by Web 2.0. In addition, *Web 2.0* makes a valuable contribution towards understanding the new developments in mobile computing as it integrates various aspects of social networking, while also tackling head-on the recent controversial debates that have arisen in a backlash to Web 2.0.

Providing valuable insight into this emerging area of the World Wide Web, *Web 2.0* is a key supplementary text for undergraduate students of media studies, sociology, philosophy and other related disciplines, as well as being an informative read for anyone with an interest in this key contemporary issue.

Sam Han is an Instructional Technology Fellow of the Macaulay Honors College at the City University of New York. He studies and writes in the fields of social and cultural theory, media studies, religion and race. He is the author of *Navigating Technomedia: Caught in the Web* (2007) and co-editor of *The Race of Time: A Charles Lemert Reader* (2009).

SHORTCUTS – *"Little Books on Big Issues"*

Shortcuts is a major new series of concise, accessible introductions to some of the major issues of our times. The series is developed as an A to Z coverage of emergent or new social, cultural and political phenomena. Issues and topics covered range from Google to global finance, from climate change to the new capitalism, from Blogs to the future of books. While the principal focus of ***Shortcuts*** is the relevance of current issues, topics, debates and thinkers to the social sciences and humanities, the books should also appeal to a wider audience seeking guidance on how to engage with today's leading social, political and philosophical debates.

Series Editor: Anthony Elliott is a social theorist, writer and Chair in the Department of Sociology at Flinders University, Australia. He is also Visiting Research Professor in the Department of Sociology at the Open University, UK, and Visiting Professor in the Department of Sociology at University College Dublin, Ireland. His writings have been published in 16 languages and he has written widely on, among other topics, identity, globalisation, society, celebrity and mobilities.

Titles in the series:

Confronting Climate Change
Constance Lever-Tracy

Feelings
Stephen Frosh

Suicide Bombings
Riaz Hassan

Web 2.0
Sam Han

Global Finance
Robert Holton

Freedom
Nick Stevenson

SHORTCUTS — *"Little Books on Big Issues"*

Series Editor's FOREWORD

New information technologies are undeniably transforming the globe as we know it and perhaps nowhere more so than with the advent of Internet-based virtuality. In **Web 2.0**, Sam Han provides a brilliant guide to the social impetuses and consequences of Web applications facilitative of information sharing and virtual communities. In this self-consciously interdisciplinary treatment of the topic, Han mixes technology and trans-nationalism, computing and commodification, hardware and software, to uncover the thrills and spills of virtuality in the era of Web 2.0. Focusing on everything from social networking sites to wikis to blogs, Han's guide to social media practices is remarkably insightful. A perfect shortcut indeed to the new informational politics.

Anthony Elliott

WEB 2.0

Sam Han

Routledge
Taylor & Francis Group

LONDON AND NEW YORK

First published 2011
by Routledge
2 Park Square, Milton Park, Abingdon, Oxon OX14 4RN

Simultaneously published in the USA and Canada
by Routledge
711 Third Avenue, New York, NY 10017

Routledge is an imprint of the Taylor & Francis Group, an informa business

British Library Cataloguing in Publication Data
A catalogue record for this book is available from the British Library

Library of Congress Cataloging in Publication Data
Han, Sam, 1984-
Web 2.0 / by Sam Han
      p.cm.
   Includes bibliographical refrences
   1. Web 2.0.   2 Social media.   I. Title.
   TK5105.88817.H35 2011
   302.23'1–dc22

                                                    2010048559

ISBN: 978–0–415–78039–1 hbk
ISBN: 978–0–415–78040–7 pbk
ISBN: 978–0–203–85522–5 ebook

Typeset in Garamond
by RefineCatch Limited, Bungay, Suffolk

Printed and bound in Great Britain by
TJ International Ltd, Padstow, Cornwall

CONTENTS

ACKNOWLEDGEMENTS

There have been numerous individuals and institutions that have supported me throughout the writing of this book. First, I want to thank Anthony Elliott, the series editor, for not only soliciting the writing of this book for Shortcuts, of which I am honored to be part, but also for the generosity and support he has shown me ever since I've known him. At Routledge, I'd like to thank Gerhard Boomgaarden, Lindsey Hall and Jennifer Dodd, who have been superb and have made the process of working on this book a breeze.

During the writing of this book, I have benefitted from an Instructional Technology Fellowship at the Macaulay Honors College of the City University of New York, where I dealt directly with many of the technologies I discuss here. At Macaulay, Joe Ugoretz deserves special mention. At Lehman College, where I did my fellowship work, I wish to acknowledge Gary Schwartz and Florence Aliberti.

At the Graduate Center, City University of New York, I would like to mention Patricia Ticineto Clough, whose work continues to inspire and influence me, especially in matters technological, and Jerry Watts, for the countless conversations and for allowing me to use office space and resources at the Institute for Research on the African Diaspora in the Americas and the Caribbean (IRADAC), of which he is director, although my work conceivably had almost nothing to do with the institute's stated intellectual aims and goals.

I'd also like to thank others who have been instrumental in my thinking about issues of this kind and others. Charles Lemert deserves particular mention, as do other members of the New York–New Haven reading group, especially Josh Scannell, Niki Achitoff-Gray and Will Runge. Thanks for letting me into the group, gang!

There has not been a shortage of friends who have emailed me articles, blog posts and the like on hearing that I was working on this book. I have no way of remembering who sent me what but there is no doubt in my mind that I have benefitted from their support. Also, albeit unorthodox, I'd like to thank the people with whom I'm "friends" on a variety of social media platforms, including those whom I've never met in person, who have also shared links.

Lastly, I'd like to acknowledge Khalia Frazier, who is with me every day in spite of the seemingly never-ending time I spend on the computer or watching TV during baseball season.

Though there are many to thank, all the shortcomings and inadequacies of this work are mine and mine alone.

Sam Han
East Harlem
New York, USA

INTRODUCTION: REMEDIATION OR CONVERGENCE?

Media and technology in the information age

In 2006 *Time Magazine* awarded its "Person of the Year" to "You." Even for those of us who couldn't care less about this kind of thing, it is obvious that "You" is not the most illustrious of choices, and, considering the magazine's previous choices, a rather unorthodox one. Past selections have ranged from Ayatollah Khomeini to Bono from U2, who along with Bill and Melinda Gates was given the honor in 2005. But when taking into account the enormous rise of the influence of new media technologies, particularly the Internet, the choice is not too surprising. The Internet has, indeed, changed many things. But what *Time*'s editorial team points to specifically by naming "You" as its person of the year is the scale of community and collaboration of knowledge that it has catalyzed, and the marked shift towards a "user-generated" technoculture, what many scholars, media executives, and journalists have called "Web 2.0."

As Lev Grossman, the author of the cover article for that issue, suggests, the Internet that has allowed "You" to win the recognition from *Time* does not resemble the Internet of the 90s' dot-com boom or the ARPANET developed by the US Department of Defense 20 years before that. In his words:

> The new Web is a very different thing. It's a tool for *bringing together* the small contributions of millions of people and making them matter ... [I]t's really a revolution ...
>
> America loves its solitary geniuses – its Einsteins, its Edisons, its Jobses – but those lonely dreamers may have to learn to play with others. Car companies are running open design contests. Reuters is carrying blog postings alongside its regular news feed. Microsoft is working overtime to fend off user-created Linux. We're looking at an explosion of productivity and innovation, and it's just getting started, as millions of minds that would otherwise have drowned in obscurity get backhauled into the global intellectual economy.
>
> *(Grossman 2006)*

Grossman identifies key trends in Web 2.0 for what he calls "the global intellectual economy." Empirically, so it seems, he is right on. Some statistics show that a blog is created every minute. Specifically, what has Grossman so excited is the potential for collective intellectual productivity. He goes so far as to call it a revolution. Although not going into the details of what technological or social transformations occurred to suggest such a thing, Grossman, I infer, is referring to the change in Internet practices from information reception to information *production* and *sharing* as exemplified by the popularity of social network sites such as Facebook and the micro-blogging services of Twitter and Tumblr, the user-generated miracle that is Wikipedia, and the ubiquity of blogs, to name just a few notable examples.

Thus, in this new era of Web 2.0, the Internet is viewed as a space of radical inclusion, a platform facilitating a veritable collaboration of ideas on a global scale, "the new digital democracy" (Grossman 2006). Now, the average Joe or Jane, instead of passively being "interpellated" into the dominant ideology, to use Marxist philosopher Louis Althusser's influential term, can contribute to this "explosion of productivity and innovation" technologically. In effect, he or she would no longer be relegated to the bottoms of the intellectual totem poles but situated well within its horizontal structure – a node in the network.

The buzz around Web 2.0 has produced a widespread notion that the Internet has blazed, and will continue to blaze, the trail in the democratization of intellectual activity and knowledge production. Indeed, there are good reasons to believe so. The explosion of the open-source model spans the deepest of nooks and crannies of the World Wide Web. This is evident in the plethora of product reviews available all over the Internet. Of course, there are the obvious places to seek them out such as Amazon and other retail websites that carry customer reviews, not to mention the thousands of blogs that are devoted to them. There is also the plethora of image databases that available for all to access. The images on Google Image Search as well as popular photo-sharing website Flickr are not only user generated but available for all who wish to download and use them.

At first glance, Web 2.0 is the becoming-social of the Web.

However, whether Web 2.0 constitutes a fundamental shift in the way the World Wide Web functions and practices taking place, this will be just one of the many themes we touch on in the course of this book. But before doing so, there must be some acknowledgement of the overall techno-social situation. To do this, we may fruitfully turn, as have many others, to the work of Manuel Castells.

In his much discussed three-volume opus *The Information Age: Economy, Society and Culture*, Castells lays out what he believes to be the fundamental aspects of the information age, and the "network society" that it spawned. Castells' trilogy, written over the course of the late 1990s and early 2000s, can be viewed largely as a capstone to the 1990s. There and in subsequent work, Castells maintains that the "new economy" of the 1990s signaled a new society, which he calls network society. The network society he contends consist of these five dimensions:

1. New technological paradigm
    Information technologies are increasingly socially embedded. One can no longer consider them to be exogenous. New information technologies allow the formation of new forms of social organization and interaction within information networks.
2. Globalization
    Globalization is the technological, organizational, and institutional capacity for various organizations to work in real time on a planetary scale.
3. The movement of culture online
    The Internet becomes the dominant frame of reference for symbolic processing from all sources and messages. Hypertext becomes the backbone of the new culture of real virtuality, in which virtuality

becomes a fundamental component of our symbolic environment, and thus of our experience as communicating beings.

4. Demise of the sovereign nation-state

This is largely a consequence of the global networks of economy, communication, knowledge and information. They are either bypassed or rearranged as central power apparatuses in networks of shared sovereignty (such as NAFTA, NATO, or EU).

5. Redefined relationship between nature and culture

As a result of increased scientific knowledge and the intimacy of humans–technologies in the information age, there is an increased ecological consciousness in the network society.

(Castells 2000, pp. 693–694)

In this litany, perhaps the most pertinent for this book are points 1 and 3 (although 2 also bears relevance). The emergence of Web 2.0 and social media can be viewed as the intensification of 1 and 3. While Castells, at the time, had to argue for the endogenous nature of information technologies, it is a claim that today would hardly be met with any kind of serious disagreement. Moreover, as social interaction increasingly takes place via media technologies—SMS texts and Twitter being some examples—then it is no surprise that culture (or what Castells rather technically deems "symbolic processing") takes place through social media.

These constitute what I'm calling the *ground* of Web 2.0.

The term "Web 2.0" emerged in 2004 when computer book publisher and open software activist Tim O'Reilly convened what he called the "Web 2.0 Conference." Whereas *Time Magazine* viewed it in terms of "democratization" of the Web, O'Reilly, and others like him, saw Web 2.0 from mostly a business orientation. As they explicitly state, "Web 2.0" was a way to reckon with the wreckage of the dot-com boom/bust of the 1990s. In a recent "white paper," a term associated with marketing and sales, called "Web Squared: Web 2.0 Five Years On," O'Reilly and John Battelle, the VP of O'Reilly Media, make the impetus behind the first Web 2.0 Conference explicit. "[It] was designed to restore confidence in an industry that had lost its way after the dotcom bust," they write.

In some ways, then, "Web 2.0" was a clever naming trick, a rebranding if you will, on behalf of the veterans of the dot-com era in the guise of a periodization scheme. According to O'Reilly, the Web of the 1990s had *content* as its defining characteristic. The new Web, Web 2.0, differs as its chief feature is sociality. Thus, if content was where capital was funneled in the 1990s, sociality was the new ground for O'Reilly and other media and technology execs to plant new seeds. The guilt-free corporate nature of the conceptualization of Web 2.0 has been the source of much discomfort for some scholars and media critics. Dutch Net critic and activist Geert Lovink, whose disdain for what he calls "Web 2.0 hype" is widely known among left-leaning media theory circles, notes, "Tag, Connect, Friend, Link, Share, Tweet. These are terms that signal any form of collective intelligence, creativity or networked socialism. They are directives from the Central Software Committee" (Lovink et al. 2009). The democratization of media and the valorization of "user-generated" culture lauded by *Time*, for Lovink, is nothing but a corporation-generated fad.

In spite of Lovink's objections (to which we will return a couple of times in subsequent chapters of this book), scholars, journalists, cultural critics, bloggers, and general observers of culture have increasingly come to agreement that there *is* indeed something new about the Web and about the *mediascape* generally since around the middle of the 2000s. They point to a "new" regime of media, identifying a new tendency in the development of software and applications on the World Wide Web but also technological devices. This has been called "social media." To describe the relationship of social media and Web 2.0, we could venture to modify Marshall McLuhan's dictum: social media are the content of Web 2.0.[1] Although the term "social media," as it is commonly understood, refers to the software, applications, and websites that constitute the entire complex of Web 2.0, I wish to extend its definition to include the technologies or devices that hook into this complex. I do this to go beyond the hegemony of the Web-centered understanding of Web 2.0.

To accuse the concept of "Web 2.0" as being Web centered may seem silly. Yet, if one thinks about what makes the complex of Web 2.0 and social media possible, that is, if one considers their "conditions of possibility," a term used frequently by scholars, we see that they are reliant on a greater technological situation—one that requires not only the applications such as Facebook and Twitter but also mobile devices such as smartphones (e.g., Apple iPhones, RIM BlackBerry), ebook readers (e.g., Amazon Kindle, Barnes & Noble nook) and netbooks, as well as the proliferation of high-speed wireless Internet in the form of Wi-Fi and

EDGE and 3G data connections. It is not simply that I wish to point out the "hardware" required for Web 2.0 and social media to function and emphasize the materiality of what many consider to be a discussion largely oriented around an assumed immateriality.[2] Rather, I am trying to suggest that Web 2.0 and social media rely on an entire network of interconnected, or potentially connectable, devices that certain platforms can run on. The World Wide Web is increasingly this platform.

Exploring whether these new devices or Web 2.0 emerged first is, in my view, a rather futile exercise. It is girded by a perspective towards studying technological change that is rooted in causality, a concept whose purchase has been on the decline in this new technological situation. This is so because whether Web 2.0 or mobile media devices came first, they enter into a complex, communicative network, whereby the idea of causality has no bearing. Web 2.0 functions under a rubric that does not privilege from where a communication originates. It does not adhere very closely to the logic of vertical control, what the French philosophers Gilles Deleuze and Felix Guattari call "arborescent." To the contrary, it is what media theorist Alex Galloway describes as "a structural form without center that resembles . . . a meshwork."

Moreover, it is not the question that I seek to raise when speaking of Web centrism. What I do mean to highlight is that Web 2.0 by its very logic goes beyond the enclosed space of a Web browser. Let us look at the case of Google Calendar, for example. In late 2006 Google announced Google Calendar, a Web application for time management, much in the style of other calendar software, like Microsoft Outlook and Apple's iCal. What made it different from these was its interoperability with mobile devices, especially smartphones. The ability to "sync" multiple devices to one's Google Calendar is one of the major reasons why it attracts users (including me). Thus, I can add "events," or calendar items, from my computer and it will show up on the calendar of my BlackBerry, and vice versa. Further, because it is a Web-based app, it can run on nearly all operating systems, as long there is some form of Internet access.

Assumed in this brief example is, of course, mobility. Increasingly, people are carrying around more and more gadgets with them. On a prominent public talk radio show in New York City, one tech blog editor said he carried at least four gadgets daily—two smartphones (one for email, the other for Web browsing), mp3 player, and FitBit Tracker, a wearable device that measures data such as the number of steps walked, quality of sleep, and other health metrics. The fact that more and more technological devices are becoming mobile, thanks to innovations that allow for extended battery life and also decrease in size, is the basis for the discourse of social media and Web 2.0.

Further, these devices are becoming more and more adept at multi-tasking. Smartphones, for instance, act not only as phones (in fact, the phone aspect of smartphones is perhaps the most underutilized of its many func-tions) but as multimedia players (video and audio), Web browsers, cameras (photographic and video), etc. To a degree, these devices are extending the logic of the computer, a machine that, since the design of the Jacquard loom, was supposed to do the work of other machines.[3] Thus, we can identify that the "computerization" of media is a necessary precondition for Web 2.0 as well. But even more generally speaking, the idea of the computer, as an abstract, meta-machine, is an important foundation not only to Web 2.0 and social media but to the general technological situation in which we find increasingly more and more functions added to smaller and smaller devices.

Recently, there have been two approaches to this new paradigm of media technologies—remediation and convergence. Jay David Bolter and Richard Grusin in *Remediation: Understanding New Media* have articulated the former, while Henry Jenkins has assessed the latter in *Convergence Culture: Where Old and New Media Collide*. These two approaches are by no means exclusive to one another in a simple, oppositional sense. They are, in my reading, complementary. Bolter and Grusin even write, "convergence is remedia-tion under another name" (Bolter & Grusin 2000, p. 224). Since both approaches are worthy of serious and sustained intellectual engagement, let us briefly look at the aspects of each that most pertain to our purposes here.

As can be gleaned from the title of their book, Bolter and Grusin are overtly playing on McLuhan's thesis on technological change. Remediation, they state, is the representation of one medium in another. Whereas he believed that old media become the content of new media, they add an additional crinkle. They suggest that remediation has a double logic. "Our culture wants both to multiply its media and to erase all traces of media-tion: ideally, it wants to erase its media in the very act of multiplying them." Thus, remediation is not only a means of looking at technological change or evolution but also a way of identifying a logic of contemporary media culture. Media technologies are self-effacing as they are multiplying.

This "double logic" can be traced throughout the history of western representation, beginning with the emergence of "perspective," which, according to the authors, is the first instance of remediation. Perspective is the remediation of immediacy. By immediacy, the authors are not describing media as a separate entity but always in relation to the human user, as an "interface." Thus, immediacy as a goal that many media technologies strive for consists of the ideal of transparency. Virtual reality (VR) technology certainly serves as an example.

Subsequent media follow in painting's footsteps in this manner. Bolter and Grusin describe it as such:

> A painting by the seventeenth-century artist Pieter Saenerdam, a photograph by Edward Weston, and a computer system for virtual reality are different in many important ways, but they are all attempts to achieve immediacy by ignoring or denying the presence of the medium and the act of mediation. All of them seek to put the viewer in the same space as the objects viewed.
>
> *(Bolter & Grusin 2000, p. 11)*

Therefore, in the remediation framework, digital media are most fruitfully understood through how they remediate—"honor, rival, and revise"— prior media, including painting, photography, film, television, and print. The idea of photorealism in the realm of computer graphics can certainly be viewed in this way. The term itself connotes that a graphic resembles a photograph. The photograph, in this formulation then, becomes the standard against which the computer graphic is measured. As Bolter and Grusin write, "in such cases, the computer is imitating not an external reality but rather another medium."

As Bolter and Grusin note, however, digital media operate under the principle of *hyper*mediacy, which they identify with the "heterogeneous 'windowed style'" of most computer operating systems. The main point of difference between the "transparent immediacy" of old (pre-digital) media and the "hypermediacy" of new (digital) media is the way in which they present visual space. In the former, space is unified, holistic and seamless. It remediates the phenomenological "experience" of consciousness. In the latter, visual space is heterogeneous. "Representation is conceived of not as a window on to the world, but rather as 'windowed' itself—with windows that open on to other media." Both types of media are striving for the same goal, which is to "get past the limits of representation and to achieve the real," though, as the authors note, they do so by quite different means. "The real" here is not meant as what theologian Paul Tillich deemed "ultimate reality," that is, an ontological category, but rather something that users will respond to emotionally.

Older, transparent media attempt this through self-effacement, by attempting to hide or recede the mediation process. The film-viewing experience of the cinema, as has been so well discussed and analyzed by feminist film theorists in particular, is a good example of a transparent medium.[4] Although films are watched in a variety of different methods, with everything from smartphones to iPods now having the capability to play back video, some readers of this book will have ventured out to the theater at some point or another. When sitting in the dark room, you will find that the giant screen takes up nearly your entire field of vision. The surround-sound technology also wraps around the viewer (literally, with the placement of the speakers). Bolter and Grusin would no doubt call this an immediate experience. The film-viewing experience is supposed to make one feel that the medium itself is not there. The size of the screen, the darkness of the room, and the volume of the sound contribute to this. Even the script of courtesy involved in film viewing, such as the turning off of mobile phones and the discouragement of talking, add to this. Transparent media rely on the unity or unbrokenness of the experience.

Newer, hypermedia do not operate within the paradigm of the unity of experience in their attempt to achieve the real. To the contrary, "digital hypermedia seek the real by multiplying mediation so as to create a feeling of fullness, a satiety of experience" (Bolter & Grusin 2000, p.53). The contemporary Web experience is perhaps the example, par excellence, of the hypermediacy. In the first place, there is no remediation of a natural, phenomenological "immediacy" or "experience as such." The experience of toggling back and forth between multiple applications and windows is quite specific to the computer. Film remediates the linear perspective of painting and photography and the computer does too, albeit with an important caveat. It can, but not exclusively. That is to say, the computer is able to remediate perspective but it is not bound to it. It can facilitate a variety of media, including but not limited to film. One's desktop (a remediation itself) can be filled with various windows open to a variety of media—photographic, video, text. Thus, hypermedia rests on a disunity of experience, of "attaining the real by filling the screen with windows" (Bolter & Grusin 2000, p.210).

Contrariwise, another framework to view the contemporary *mediascape* that has emerged in recent years is "convergence." The media analyst most closely associated with convergence is Henry Jenkins, who founded the Comparative Media Studies program at the Massachusetts Institute of Technology. In his *Convergence Culture*, Jenkins lays out several aspects of not only technological convergence but what he calls "convergence *culture*," which he argues has pervaded not only the way in which media technologies function but also how business and fan culture works. As he writes, "convergence represents a cultural shift as consumers are encouraged to seek out new information and make connections among dispersed media content" (Jenkins 2006, p.3).

Against the business-oriented definition of convergence that assumed old media would be wholly subsumed by new media—a complete reme-diation of sorts, which places the future of the entertainment and news industries hanging on convergence, Jenkins defines it as such:

> . . . the flow of content across multiple media platforms, the cooper-ation between multiple media industries, and the migratory behavior of media audiences who will go almost anywhere in search of the kinds of entertainment experiences they want.
>
> *(Jenkins 2006, p.2)*

The most important "lesson" of convergence, according to him, is in this realm of media evolution. New media did not replace old media but rather "enabled the same content to flow through many different channels and assume many different forms at the point of reception" (Jenkins 2006, p.11). In the convergence paradigm, old media and new media will interact in a more complicated fashion. Thus:

> Media convergence is more than simply a technological shift. Convergence alters the relationship between existing technologies, industries, markets, genres, and audiences. Convergence alters the logic by which media industries operate and by which media consumers process news and entertainment. Keep this in mind: convergence refers to a process, not an endpoint.
>
> *(Jenkins 2006, p.16)*

Although convergence is the cultural logic of media today, Jenkins provides two other concepts on whose cooperation convergence culture relies—participatory culture and collective intelligence.

The fast circulation of media content, a foundational attribute of "convergence culture" (as well as social media and Web 2.0), depends on the active participation of users. It is reliant on the diminishing distinction of consumer and producer, seeing them as "participants who interact with each other according to a new set of rules that none of us quite fully understands" (Jenkins 2006, p.3).

Collective intelligence refers to the way users extract from the flow of information. Since there is always at one time more information than a normal human brain can retain and process, the "consumption" of information becomes a collective experience. As he puts it, "because there is more information on any given topic than anyone can store in their head, there is an added incentive for us to talk among ourselves about the media we consume" (Jenkins 2006, p.4).

However, as Jenkins reminds, old paradigms die hard, especially in the tech world, where the ideology of the "digital revolution" propagated a theory of capital-P Progress, whereby one dominant technology (radio, for example) is replaced by another (television). Hence, one of the major fallacies around the discourse of "convergence," especially as the business world has construed it, is what Jenkins calls the "Black Box fallacy" (Jenkins 2006, p.16). The Black Box fallacy is the idea that has circulated around tech business circles that sees the coming of a singular device that incorporates nearly every technological process. This, Jenkins notes, is not only a pipe dream but also a wholly technological view of social change. It does not take into consideration changes outside technology that may influence or may interact with developments within it. But as Jenkins makes clear, when looking at the evolution of media technologies "each old medium was forced to coexist with the emerging media" (Jenkins 2006, p.14). There was *never* a clean, linear replacement of one medium or regime of media with another.

One of the places where the convergence culture is most notably present is in the realm of fan culture. Jenkins, an early scholar of fan culture,[5] looks at what he calls the "Harry Potter Wars." This term refers to a series of events that took place in response to the emergence of fan fiction, fictional writings made by fans using the language and characters of the global sensation book series by J.K. Rowling. Much of the circulation of these materials occurred on the Web on fan sites such as *The Daily Prophet*, started by a 13-year-old Heather Lawver. *The Daily Prophet* is a school newspaper for Hogwarts, the school that Harry and his friends attend in the book series. It collects stories from all over the world, at one point boasting 102 contributors. Rowling and her publishers initially encouraged this kind of fandom. (Jenkins calls the practice of taking the content of one medium and remixing it for another, "transmedia storytelling.") But when Warner Brothers bought the film, they sought to take control of the fan sites' domain names and content. After Lawver was able to wage a major media campaign, with large support of the Harry Potter fan community, Warner Brothers backed down, admitting their mistake (Jenkins 2006, p.188).

For Jenkins, this episode highlights a few interesting issues relating to convergence today. First, it reveals the lag that exists between the law and media culture. Copyright law in particular has not yet caught up with the cultural practices of the day, most of which are taking place with some form of digital technology and shared through the Web. Fan fiction exists in a legal grey zone. "Current copyright law simply doesn't have a category for dealing with amateur creative expression," he writes. In turn, the idea of "authorship" is hotly contested. On the one hand, as Walter Benjamin would put it, fan communities, and fan fiction in particular, strip away the aura of the creative process.[6] On the other hand, many more people as fans feel that their contributions are as original as the source material from which they draw and can claim authorship. On the whole, however, Jenkins maintains, the creative process is "demystified," opening up spaces for communal modes of expression, as opposed to the individualized, western idea of "the author."[7]

But most importantly for Jenkins, this episode signals that media convergence has facilitated a deep learning culture that is unofficial and inter-generational. The learning culture of the fan community of Harry Potter is, as he says, an "affinity space," drawing from Paul Gee.

> Affinity spaces offer powerful opportunities for learning, Gee argues, because they are sustained by common endeavors that bridge across differences in age, class, race, gender and educational level, because people can participate in various ways according to their skills and interests, because they depend on peer-to-peer

teaching with each participant constantly motivated to acquire new knowledge or refine his or her existing skills, and because they allow each participant to feel like an expert while tapping the expertise of others.

(Jenkins 2006, p.177)

The fan fiction produced by Lawver and others like her sit at the nexus of participatory culture and collective intelligence, signaling a new kind of learning and mode of cultural practice facilitated by media convergence. Convergence culture is based on a new kind of media literacy, a new set of skills that are required for people to become full participants in convergent culture—the ability to pool knowledge with others in a collaborative enterprise and the ability to circulate what you create via the Internet so that it can be shared with others (Jenkins 2006, p.176).

Thus, convergence is not simply a technological matter; it is the becoming-social of the World Wide Web. It is the move away from medium specificity to true multimedia content. It is a move "toward the increased interdependence of communications systems, toward multiple ways of accessing media content, and toward ever more complex relations between top-down corporate media and bottom-up participatory culture" (Jenkins 2006, p.243). In spite of the rather positive implications of convergence for fan culture, for instance, there are, as Jenkins right notes, ways in which convergence could be viewed as simply another corporate means by which to, if not shape consumer behavior, then to analyze it in order to shape it. However, in spite of this interconnection of corporate media and participatory culture, on the whole, for Jenkins, opens up a space for rerouting power from the corporate media. For one thing, participation has become part of the "normal ways that media operate" (Jenkins 2006, p.246). Whereas traditional, mass media tended towards "officialization," the participatory nature of convergence culture undermines such a dynamic, allowing for great participation but also cultural diversity.

Remediation and convergence, then, are two complementary ways in which to view the techno-cultural conditions by which Web 2.0 exists today. It exists and flourishes only to the extent in which it branches outside itself and extends beyond the confines of the Web. Perhaps this is the paradox of Web 2.0: it must not stay within the "space" of the Web but relies on its extension and distribution.

We can then cautiously state that the following are the points most emphasized about the contemporary *mediascape*, as articulated by both convergence and remediation, as they relate in particular to Web 2.0. They constitute, to use an academic term, the *field*,[8] the technological, social and cultural infrastructure within which the ideas, discourses, and practices surrounding Web 2.0 exist.

1. Media technologies multiply. As they do, unlike the transparent media of the past, they make their interfaces a selling point. They do not try to efface the process of mediation but, in fact, highlight it.
2. As they evolve, they remediate prior media technologies. This development, however, is not be linear. It will depend on the reception and use of new devices and media, and thus take on unexpected turns.
3. Content will continue to flow through more and more channels, though they will continue to use the Internet as the main platform for these channels. For this to be possible, there must be increased cooperation between media industries to create interoperable technologies, devices that can communicate with one another.
4. Users will continue to be producers as well consumers. The boundary between production and consumption will further dissolve.
5. The sharing of information, "linking" in Net lingo, is a widespread value.

Overview of the book

In Chapter 1, I provide a brief overview of the history of the World Wide Web. In doing so, I attempt to make clear a difference that many who are semi-experts do not generally maintain—that of the Internet as opposed to the World Wide Web. By providing a brief history of the World Wide Web, I attempt to contextualize the "Web" portion of "Web 2.0." In the following chapter, I delve into the "2.0" of the "Web 2.0." I discuss what various media analysts, scholars, and pundits have identified as aspects particular to the current instantiation of the World Wide Web, focusing on social media practices such as blogging and photo sharing. In Chapter 3, I deal with the consequences of social networking, taking stock of the type of sociality that is representative of Web 2.0. I then move on to a phenomenology of the mobile computing experience that traverses the separation of on- and offline interactions in Chapter 4. Here, I attempt to give an account of the hardware that facilitates the mobility and integrative nature of computing in the era of Web 2.0. In the final chapter, I address some of the major articulations of the backlash against Web 2.0, using the framework of what I call "informational politics."

Due to constraints of space, I have not been able to delve into the technical and theoretical minutiae of the themes touched on throughout this book. It is for this reason that we have included an annotated list of some works, links, and names of writers, which may be of some help to those readers who wish I had addressed a particular topic more. One word of warning, however: the seemingly ever-changing nature of the World Wide Web, and technology in general, makes it very difficult to point to *loci classici*, that is, works that are widely agreed on as the pre-eminent tomes on a subject. Ask any university instructor trying to construct a reading list for a course on Internet studies or sociology of media. For this reason, the list will be obsolesced almost as soon as it is published. "So it goes," as the great twentieth-century American novelist Kurt Vonnegut refrained. Yet, for those for whom this book is really their true introduction to new media studies or social/cultural studies of technology, the "Weblography" will be, I hope, of some use.

Notes

1 Marshall McLuhan, perhaps the most well-known North American media theorist, stated that the content of a new medium is an old medium. This has been the basis for much of media theory since then. See McLuhan, M., 1964. *Understanding Media: The Extensions of Man*, Signet.
2 This has been largely the project of German media theorist Friedrich Kittler, who argues that that there is no software. See his Kittler, F., 2005. There is No Software, CTheory.net. Available at: http://www.ctheory.net/articles.aspx?id = 74. [Accessed March 4, 2010].
3 The Jacquard loom is usually given credit as the first theoretical computer. Although Charles Babbage would later take its punch-card system to create the analytical engine, the Jacquard loom is nevertheless the widely accepted "first" computer in the history of computing. See Plant, S., 1997. *Zeros + Ones*, Doubleday.
4 There are too many titles in the realm of which I speak to list here, but a standout among them is Rose, J., 2005. *Sexuality in the Field of Vision*, Verso. A critical summary of developments in feminist film studies can be found in Clough, P.T., 1994. *Feminist Thought: Desire, Power, and Academic Discourse*, Blackwell.

5 See Jenkins, H., 1992. *Textual Poachers: Television Fans and Participatory Culture*, Routledge.
6 Walter Benjamin famously hinted at the "end of aura" due to mechanical reproduction. See Benjamin, W. & Arendt, H., 1969. The Work of Art in the Age of Mechanical Reproduction. In *Illuminations*, Schocken Books.
7 There have been numerous debates in literary theory over the figure of the author. Two places among many to start at are Foucault, M., 1984. What is an Author? In *The Foucault Reader*, Vintage; and Barthes, R. & Heath, S., 1978. The Death of the Author. In *Image, Music, Text*, Macmillan.
8 Sociologist Pierre Bourdieu has provided a robust theory of "field" or *champ*, which he suggests is a sort of matrix of rules, institutions, and categories that delimit and/or engender certain formations of thought and action. Although he does not define it in any declarative sense, he uses it as an analytic for investigation most proficiently, in my opinion, in Bourdieu, P., 1993. *The Field of Cultural Production*, Columbia University Press.

References

Barthes, R. & Heath, S., 1978. The Death of the Author. In *Image, Music, Text*, Macmillan.

Benjamin, W. & Arendt, H., 1969. The Work of Art in the Age of Mechanical Reproduction. In *Illuminations*, Schocken Books.

Bolter, J.D. & Grusin, R., 2000. *Remediation: Understanding New Media* 1st edn, MIT Press.

Bourdieu, P., 1993. *The Field of Cultural Production*, Columbia University Press.

Castells, M., 2000. Toward a Sociology of the Network Society, *Contemporary Sociology*, 29(5), 693–99.

Clough, P.T., 1994. *Feminist Thought: Desire, Power, and Academic Discourse*, Blackwell.

Foucault, M., 1984. What is an Author? In *The Foucault Reader*, Vintage.

Galloway, A.R., 2004. *Protocol*, MIT Press.

Grossman, L., 2006. Time's Person of the Year: You, *Time*. Available at: http://www.time.com/time/magazine/article/0,9171,1569514,00.html. [Accessed March 3, 2010.]

Jenkins, H., 2006. *Convergence Culture: Where Old and New Media Collide* illustrated edn, New York University Press.

——, 1992. *Textual Poachers: Television Fans and Participatory Culture*, Routledge.

Kittler, F., 2005. There is No Software, *CTheory.net*. Available at: http://www.ctheory.net/articles.aspx?id=74. [Accessed March 4, 2010.]

Lehrer, B., 2010. Inspector Gadget: Over-Deviced (March 04, 2010), *The Brian Lehrer Show*. Available at: http://www.wnyc.org/shows/bl/episodes/2010/03/04/segments/151129. [Accessed March 4, 2010.]

Leiner, B., Cerf, V.G., Clark, D.D., Kahn, R.E., Kleinrock, L., Lynch, D.C., et al., 2003. A Brief History of the Internet, *Internet Society*. Available at: http://www.isoc.org/internet/history/brief.shtml. [Accessed April 15, 2010.]

Lovink, G., Rossiter, N., & Ippolita, 2009. < nettime > The Digital Given – 10 Web 2.0 Theses by Ippolita, Geert Lovink, *Nettime Mailing List Archives*. Available at: http://www.nettime.org/Lists-Archives/nettime-l-0906/msg00028.html. [Accessed March 3, 2010.]

McLuhan, M., 1964. *Understanding Media: The Extensions of Man*, Signet.

Myers, R., 2010. The GNU Operating System, *GNU Operating System*. Available at: http://www.gnu.org/. [Accessed May 17, 2010.]

O'Reilly, T. & Battelle, J., 2009. Web Squared: Web 2.0 Five Years On, *Web 2.0 Summit*. Available at: http://www.web2summit.com/web2009/public/schedule/detail/10194. [Accessed March 3, 2010.]

Rose, J., 2005. *Sexuality in the Field of Vision*, Verso.

1

WHAT IS THE "WEB" IN "WEB 2.0"?

A short history of the Web

Today, many people use the terms "Web" (short for World Wide Web), "Internet," or "online" interchangeably. "I got this song online." "I got this from the Internet." "It's from the Web." These all work. They do a good enough job of conveying the meaning of the speaker. The terms World Wide and the Internet, although they are related, are distinct technical entities; as phenomena in the computing experience for most users, however, this is of little consequence. One of the aims of this chapter will be to make this distinction clearer and also argue for its significance.

It may be helpful to think of the Web as a part of the Internet. The Web is a set of hyperlinked documents and pages *on* the Internet. This is most intuitively understood by looking at the URL of any given website or blog. Most Web addresses use hypertext transfer protocol (HTTP). On occasion, some users of the Internet, especially those who are proficient enough to manage their own websites or blogs, have to upload files to their site or blog, and must access an address using the file transfer protocol (FTP). These two protocols are part of what is called the application layer of the Internet protocol suite, alternatively called TCP/IP (transmission protocol/Internet protocol). While space does not permit delving more deeply into the intricacies of these various protocols, it is important to note that "the Internet" is more than what exists within the rectangular frame of the Web browser. There is a complex architecture underneath it all. If looking at the World Wide Web as being a part, but not a component or element of the Internet is not the best illustration, perhaps we can say that the Web is one way of *experiencing* the Internet. Think of the Web as being the top-most layer. It is how most proficient but not expert users experience the Web. It is like an island, which, in spite of appearing as if floating on the water, extends down to the ocean floor.

Behind the situation that occurs today, i.e., where the "Web" is equated to the "Internet," there lies a complicated history. To detail it and do it justice would take an entire book. The aim of this chapter is to condense the most important aspects of this rather complex history and extract certain moments that are particularly important for the topic of this book—Web 2.0. Although it is arguable that all developments in the history of the Internet and the World Wide Web contribute to the current regime of social media, we would contend that there are specific moments that are more important than others.

The overarching aim of this chapter will be to give a brief history of the World Wide Web and the Internet, and to situate Web 2.0 within this trajectory. To accomplish this, we begin with a brief "pre-history" of the World Wide Web, detailing the Internet prior to the visual interface known as the browser. We then move on to the history of the World Wide Web (the "Internet" as most of us know it). Here, we spend time highlighting some of the technical and experiential (or user) differences between Web 1.0 and Web 2.0. We conclude with a brief assessment of the open-source movement, looking especially at Wikipedia, which has most often been identified as embodying open source *and* Web 2.0, par excellence.

A pre-history of the World Wide Web

The World Wide Web is a graphical interface for the Internet. Prior to the graphical interface and the use of browsers, such as Internet Explorer, Mozilla Firefox, and Google Chrome, the Internet was accessed mostly through something like Telnet (short for terminal network), a text-based network protocol that allowed for bidirectional communication, which looks a lot like MS-DOS because of its command-line interface. (See Figure 1.1.) It looked *very* different from the Web that we are used to today.

FIGURE 1.1 Telnet, one of the first graphical interfaces (Source: ona1a [http://www.flickr.com/photos/ona1a/]).

This blackbox, which by today's standard would be the very definition of poor user interface in the terminology of human–computer interaction (HCI), is nevertheless one of the first graphical interfaces, although in most histories of the Internet and the World Wide Web, "graphical" refers to entrance of images and video (not text) on a Web page.

The history of the Internet, therefore, reaches further back than that of the Web. Although there is some disagreement on the matter, many scholars and journalists alike place the date of the "inception" of the Internet to 1969. On 2 September 1969 two computers on the campus of UCLA transmitted data back and forth on cable. A month later the computers from UCLA connected with those 300 miles away in Stanford. This is the beginning of the ARPANET, a network that was supposed to link different researchers around the USA who were working on projects for the Pentagon. ARPA stands for Advanced Research Projects Agency, a wing of the Department of Defense.[1]

The idea of the interconnected networks, however, had existed since at least J.C.R. Licklider's memos on what he called "Intergalactic Computer

Network" published throughout the 1960s. Licklider, a computer scientist at the Massachusetts Institute of Technology and also the first head of the information processing office of ARPA, wrote of a global network of computers that would allow users to access data and programs from any point in the network. The implementation of packet switching aided the actualization of Licklider's vision of the computer as a *communicative* device occurred with the successful establishment of the ARPANET network, which eventually added UC-Santa Barbara and University of Utah to the mix.[2]

The computers in the ARPANET network were able to communicate, that is, transmit data, with one another through something called "packet switching." Simply, packet switching is a means of slicing data of all kinds (text, graphics, audio or video) into discrete blocks. The network can route the blocks independently of one another, depending on the resources available at that moment. Packet switching is advantageous because of its efficiency; that is to say, it makes the best use of the capacities of all of the links in the network. More importantly, it ensures that the message will always get through since there are so many different routes a single packet can take. This is in direct opposition to previous a form of networking, circuit switching, which could not send the message successfully if there were a problem with one.[3]

Additionally, an important advantage of packet switching was that it embodied a concept known as open architecture. Open architecture is an idea that allows for various networks to connect with each other, in spite of their particularities. In an open-architecture network, networks did not need to be designed under a single rubric but could be individually designed and developed. *Net*works could be *inter*connected without a hierarchical relationship. Open architecture made it so that identity was not the condition of possibility for communication but allowed for difference. Therefore, networks that were not necessarily created, designed, and maintained by ARPA could, in theory, connect with it. But this is not as easy as it sounds, especially for those of us who have grown up in the era of technomedia, where basic amount interoperability is not only expected but also crucial.[4] In 1972, Robert Kahn and Vinton Cerf solved this by moving the responsibility of controlling how, and checking whether, packets had been transmitted from the software in the network to software on computers that were sending and receiving packets. Although this was a relatively small tweak, it had major consequences, building the foundation for what is today called TCP/IP. "[N]etworks of one sort or another all became simply pieces of wire for carrying data. To packets of data squirted into them, the various networks all looked and behaved the same" (*Economist* 2009).

From this followed various developments in Internet use, which are significant for how we use and think about the Internet today. The most significant is perhaps the advent of email, developed by Ray Tomlinson, who first decided to use the @ symbol to divide the user name from the computer name, which later became the *domain* name. Another, just as important development is the use of the Internet for content storage. Project Gutenberg began to store entire books and documents in the public domain available electronically. Email and Project Gutenberg are significant moments in the pre-history of the World Wide Web.

Additionally, there was the introduction of the Bulletin Board System (BBS), the first discussion forum in 1978, as well as the first Multiuser Dungeon (MUD). This of course led to other virtual communities such as Whole Earth 'Lectronic Link, simply the WELL.[5] A decade later came the Internet Relay Chat (IRC), a precursor to chat rooms and instant messaging, which allowed for real-time, synchronous messaging. Further, it also allowed for data transfers, which could be viewed as a primitive form of peer-to-peer networks in the vein of Napster. Although they preceded the Web proper, they were nevertheless harbingers of how the Web would be used—for communication and information search.

The emergence of the World Wide Web

In 1989, Tim Berners-Lee at the European Centre for Nuclear Research (CERN) drafted a paper titled "Information Management: A Proposal." In it, he visualized a model for how to manage the utterly immense amount of information for various projects at CERN. The idea was to convince CERN of the benefits of adopting a global hypertext system, which had been developed by Doug Engelbart in the 1960s, to manage information. CERN approved his proposal and by 1991, along with his colleague Robert Cailliau, Berners-Lee had written the basics of a hypertext graphical user interface (GUI), using software called NeXTStep. The rudimentary elements of this code are still used by Web designers today—HTML, HTTP, and URLs. He named it "WorldWideWeb." The first Web page was, indeed, a page explaining the Web.

The mid-1990s signaled the explosion of the World Wide Web into the mainstream, with the development of the first graphical Web browser available to the public, Mosaic, which was quickly followed by Netscape Navigator. Many business observers have identified the period of the 1995–2000 as the dot-com or IT bubble. Castells has alternatively called it the IT revolution of the 1990s. In this period, we saw the takeoff of a variety of internet service providers, including America Online, Compuserve, and Prodigy. Their incredible rise was intimately bound to the popularization of the personal computer, which by the 1990s had reduced in price and in size significantly enough where households were beginning to purchase them, not just offices. Importantly, these personal computers also came with a modem, which allowed the computer to connect to the Internet through a telephone line. By the mid-to-late 1990s, websites had become a common feature of many business and organizations. With the launch of Geocities, individuals could have their own Web pages. This is particularly important as individuals and business were virtually on the same footing when producing content for the Web. Not long after this event, personal Web pages would turn into online diaries or Web logs (or just blogs), with services such as Xanga LiveJournal, which allowed for the creation of a blog with minimal technical expertise. Web-based email came not much longer afterwards with Hotmail. Although search engines had existed prior to it, Google's emergence marked a key moment for the early Web.

As you can see, the Web represents two things in the history of the Internet. For one, it is the remediation of the Internet. Various aspects of the Internet, including email and virtual communities, were remediated onto the Web. This may sound as if we are underplaying the significance of this fact but quite the contrary: the movement of these various functions to the World Wide Web is something like a massification of the Internet. To be clear, this is not to say that the World Wide Web popularized the Internet on its own. But it did provide a means for non-experts to get online. This was, as mentioned earlier, aided by the decline in price of personal computers. Nevertheless, prior to the Web and the Web browser, the Internet was for those with the means and the knowledge to be able to use them. It was an "expert system" (Giddens) par excellence. The Web allowed for those with basic computing skills and familiarity with the interface of the desktop.

The World Wide Web, up until the dot-com bust of 2001, could be seen as engendering a certain set of values for its users. That is to say, the Web in this period was used mainly as an information culler. An early ISP, Prodigy, in particular, called itself the first consumer online service, since it offered an intuitive graphical user interface. But the main uses of Prodigy were to receive information—weather, sports scores, stock information. Although there was undoubtedly "interactivity," which had separated the Internet and the Web from prior media, there was no "content creation." Users of the Web could interact with one another and partake in chat rooms and discussion threads, and have encyclopedic information at the touch of their fingertips. "Web 1.0," then, can be characterized by information *consumption*.

We hesitantly label this period Web 1.0 since it gives the air of linear progress, making the years leading up to the end of the millennium as some kind of precursor to the messianic appearance of the social Web.

This is far from the case.

There are plenty of products, services, and trends dominant during the 1990s that are merely figments of the imagination for those of us who were actively on the Web at the time. The chat room is the butt end of jokes today. Blog comment sections have overtaken discussion forums. The "becoming-social" of the Web is not, we would suggest, the sole actualization of an intrinsic social nature of the World Wide Web. While it is undoubtedly the case that the Web and the Internet generally have always had a social aspect, Web 2.0 is a phenomenon that can best be explained as a confluence of commercial interests, the technological bias towards sociality intrinsic to the Internet, and the always unexpected ways in which people create new ways of using technology, which were either unforeseen by their developers or even forbidden.

One such case is, of course, file sharing. With the rise of Napster, famously created by a college student in 1998, the term "piracy" instantaneously became associated with the Internet. Although Napster was *not* Web based, since it was a standalone application that connected different computers via the Internet, allowing various computers to share certain files (mostly music files), it is certainly an important moment in the later development of Web 2.0, as it served as a lightning rod, marking a division among media critics, legal scholars, and corporations as to who was for and who was against file sharing.[6] Napster, and the whole movement of file sharing, is an important moment in the pre-history of Web 2.0. Having come about a couple of years "before" the open-source movement (since the World Wide Web and the Internet were open source prior to the period of commercialization and corporatization that we refer to as the dot-com bubble), file sharing is an early instance of what we consider a new system of values (and indeed value, in the economic sense). Sharing became a premium in file sharing culture. In fact, in some file-sharing networks, the more one shared, that is, allowed other members of the network to download their music collection, the faster one's downloads went. Although this is but one example, the culture of file sharing was in no small part influential on the open-source movement, which, with the launch of Wikipedia, gained great attention.

The seeds of Web 2.0: Wikipedia and open source

Wikipedia may be viewed as the symbolic beginning of Web 2.0. It is admittedly an easy marker. But we risk calling it so because it embodies so many of the chief tenets of the open-source movement. Although we deal with the open-source movement in greater detail in the next chapter, it is the explicit championing of the spirit of collaboration by the open-source movement that Wikipedia embodies that we wish to spend time on. Wikipedia, and its beginnings, function as somewhat of an allegory of Web 2.0, as it has been described by many unofficial histories of the World Wide Web and the Internet more broadly as paving the way for "collective Web content generation" and "social media," two of the most significant aspects of Web 2.0.

Jimmy Wales and Larry Sanger founded Wikipedia in 2001, in the wake of the dot-com bubble. Previously, Wales and Sanger were working on Nupedia, an encyclopedia project that was based on the traditional model of entries written by experts, which was, however, like its successor Wikipedia, free and Web based. It was to generate revenue through the ad-based model that the many websites that give away content for free, such as those of some major national newspapers, today rely on. Nupedia, though free and Web based, was not the only free encyclopedia project around on the Web. There was also GNUpedia, which was quite similar to scope and vision of Nupedia but was under the auspices of programmer/ activist Richard Stallman and his Free Software Foundation. GNUpedia, later renamed GNE, was based on GNU, "a Unix-like operating system which is free software." (Many users of GNU today use it in modified form known as Linux.) Wikipedia would eventually take over the operations of GNUpedia, scrap Nupedia, and use GNUpedia's GNU Free Documentation License.

What was novel about GNUpedia, or the Free Universal Encyclopedia and Learning Resource as it was called, was, under Stallman's vision, a direct alternative to what he saw as the impending corporatization of knowledge:

> The World Wide Web has the potential to develop into a universal encyclopedia covering all areas of knowledge, and a complete library of instructional courses. This outcome could happen without any special effort, if no one interferes. But corporations are mobilizing now to direct the future down a different track—one in which they control and restrict access to learning materials, so as to extract money from people who want to learn.
>
> *(Stallman 2000)*

These words, from Stallman's initial announcement email, reveal some of the ideological ground on which Wikipedia operated. Stallman gave the following criteria for the universal free encyclopedia:

*   The free encyclopedia should be open to public access by everyone who can gain access to the Web.
*   Therefore, each encyclopedia article and each course should explicitly grant irrevocable permission for anyone to make verbatim copies available on mirror sites. This permission should be one of the basic stated principles of the free encyclopedia.
*   Therefore, we must adopt a basic rule that anyone is permitted to publish an accurate translation of any article or course, with proper attribution. Each article and each course should carry a statement giving permission for translations.
*   Each encyclopedia article or course should permit anyone to quote arbitrary portions in another encyclopedia article or course, provided

proper attribution is given. This will make it possible to build on the work others have done, without the need to completely replace it.

• There will be no single organization in charge of what to include in the encyclopedia or the learning resource, no one that can be lobbied to exclude "creation science" or holocaust denial (or, by the same token, lobbied to exclude evolution or the history of Nazi death camps). Where there is controversy, multiple views will be represented. So it will be useful for readers to be able to see who endorses or has reviewed a given article's version of the subject.

(Stallman 2000)

This list contains many of the key tenets of Wikipedia, which is unsurprising since Stallman later endorsed it after GNUPedia failed to take off. (GNUPedia, in response, changed its name to GNE—GNE is Not an Encyclopedia—and reframed itself as a library of opinions and general knowledge base.)

Wikipedia attracted vast amounts of attention for several years after its 2001 launch, most notably in 2007, when its English version reached over 2 million entries, making it the largest encyclopedia ever assembled in recorded history. Much of the mainstream media attention that it received at the time reflected a general wonderment for "open source," a set of practices for collaborative computer programming and Web development that had been around since 1998 (although the idea of sharing ideas and collaborative projects has been around since the birth of writing, it could be argued). Wikipedia, in the new media at least, became representative of what would turn out to be a rather nebulous signifier, as the title of a newspaper article in 2005 on some of the misinformation on Wikipedia makes clear, "Wikipedia: Open-source, and Open to Abuse." "Open source" became conflated with "peer production" and "crowd sourcing," which, judging from the brief history provided earlier, had been occurring since the inception of the World Wide Web. But the prospects of having a successful enterprise such as Wikipedia entranced much of the media coverage so as to spark a retort by Wikipedia to correct some of the media portrayals, some of which were highly complimentary. In a 2007 *New York Times Magazine* article on his home, Wikipedia founder Wales stated that the greatest misconception about Wikipedia was that it was democratic. "We aren't democratic," he says. "Our readers edit the entries, but we're actually quite snobby. The core community appreciates when someone is knowledgeable, and thinks some people are idiots and shouldn't be writing."

Wikipedia, therefore, according to its own founder, was not as "open" as people thought it was. In spite of this "walking back" by Wales, there is, nevertheless, a demonstrable line that can be drawn between the open-source movement and Wikipedia. Let us spend some time on what exactly "open source" is and what its implications for Web 2.0 are.

One of the most well-known proponents and spokesman of the open-source and free software movement is Eric Steven Raymond, who wrote *The Cathedral and the Bazaar*, which is widely accepted as the *95 Theses* of the open-source movement. First delivered as a talk for a conference of Linux (itself one of the earliest examples of open-source software) users and developers, the manifesto, if you will, is a telling of Raymond's experience of developing an email client in what he calls the "bazaar" model. Most simply, the bazaar model can be understood by Raymond's description of Linux, which he identifies as what "converted" him from being a cathedral-minded software engineer to a bazaar-minded software engineer. The bazaar model is based on what Raymond calls "Linus' Law," a term named after Linus Torvalds' style of development for the Linux operating system, of which Torvalds wrote the kernel. Torvalds, a Finnish software engineer, had a unique philosophy in developing Linux: "release early and often, delegate everything you can, be open to the point of promiscuity." The promiscuousness of Linux resulted in:

> a world-class operating system [coalesced] as if by magic out of part-time hacking by several thousand developers scattered all over the planet, connected only by the tenuous strands of the Internet . . . No quiet, reverent cathedral-building here—rather, the Linux community seemed to resemble a great babbling bazaar of differing agendas and approaches (aptly symbolized by the Linux archive sites, who'd take submission from *anyone*) out of which a coherent and stable system could seemingly emerge only by a succession of miracles.
>
> *(Raymond 2002)*

In the course of his essay, Raymond formulates aphorisms for open-source development, while giving an account of his own attempt at implementing Linus' Law in "hacking" a mail client for email.[7] It is not in the scope of this book to go through each one but let us look at some of the ones that bear particular relevance to what would later be called the open-source movement:

1. Every good work of software starts by scratching a developer's personal itch.
2. Good programmers know what to write. Great ones know what to rewrite (and reuse).
3. Treating your users as co-developers is your least-hassle route to rapid code improvement and effective debugging.
4. Release early. Release often. And listen to your customers.
5. Given a large enough beta-tester and co-developer base, almost every problem will be characterized quickly and the fix obvious to someone.
6. The next best thing to having good ideas is recognizing good ideas from your users. Sometimes the latter is better.

Although this list of aphorisms is highly abridged, the striking feature about it is that it closely mirrors the ideological and practical basis of much of Web 2.0, as the emphasis on user feedback, collective troubleshooting, code recycling, and beta releasing make clear. These aphorisms are woven with the common thread of the truism that the collective always does better than the individual. As Raymond argues, what drives open-source software is not only the creative investment of the code writer (or software engineer) but the use of already existing code. This requires then a non-proprietary, or "non-territorial" as Raymond describes it, outlook on software and the enterprise of writing code. In addition, the code benefits from many sets of eyes especially as most software releases are usually not bug free. What opening the source code for software does is it expands the talent pool, allowing for not only debugging but also the improvement of the software itself as many programmers, in their use of the software, find different functionality issues than others. "More users find more bugs."

Further, Raymond also highlights the importance of frequent updates to releases. In the virus-laden computing world of today, the frequent updating of software is quite common. But when Raymond was writing *The Cathedral and the Bazaar*, frequent releases were seen as potential sources of embarrassment. Common (read: corporate) wisdom at the time stated that buggy software releases would repel users. However, as Raymond argues, this was not the case for the mail client he was working on—

Fetchmail. For him, the users remained and, because they invested in the software, they became "co-developers."

Therefore, the success of open source, for Raymond, was due to the bazaar model of an expanded pool of talent made up of a voluntary community of interest. This he believed was reflective of a new incentive structure and regime of institutional control, one that shirked the conventional model of centralized management. Raymond goes so far as to suggest that open source is the future not because it is inherently better but because the closed-source model cannot evolve rapidly enough "to win an evolutionary arms race."

This theme of evolution was also the subject of Clay Shirky's 1996 essay "In Praise of Evolvable Systems." Shirky, writer and teacher of new technologies, has long heralded the collaborative potential of the Internet. In this early essay, he explains the success of the World Wide Web, suggesting that it is remarkable that something so poorly designed became "the Next Big Thing." As he notes, the Web was "infuriating" to serious practitioners, who went so far as to call HTML and HTTP, respectively, the Whoopee Cushion and Joy Buzzer of Internet protocols.

He points to two Internet protocols in the early 1990s, Gopher and Wide Area Information Server. These were "strong—carefully thought-out, painstakingly implemented, self-consistent and centrally designed. Each had the backing of serious academic research, and each was rapidly gaining adherents." Moreover, beyond the Internet were other protocols such as CD-ROMS, which were also similarly designed. These all had a few things in common. They all had major institutional support, either from corporations or from educational institutions. Additionally, and most importantly, they were internally cohesive, each operating "in a kind of hermetically sealed environment where it interacted not at all with its neighbors" (Shirky 1996). This lack of interoperability directly contributed to the demise of some of these media, and their failure to become "industry standards."

The case of the rise of the Web is indicative of the overturning of this centralization. What was at one point seen as a "weakness" became strength for the future:

> The Web, in its earliest conception, was nothing more than a series of pointers. It grew not out of a desire to be an electronic encyclopedia

so much as an electronic Post-it note. The idea of keeping pointers to
ftp sites, Gopher indices, Veronica search engines and so forth all in
one place doesn't seem so remarkable now, but in fact it was the one
thing missing from the growing welter of different protocols, each of
which was too strong to interoperate well with the others.

(Shirky 1996)

It is because of the Web's evolvability and its functionality not being
sacrificed by its interoperability that it was able to take off in such a way,
according to Shirky. Systems that "proceed not under the sole direction of
one centralized design authority but by being adapted and extended in a
thousand small ways in a thousand places at once" succeed (Shirky 1996).
Like Raymond's aphorisms, Shirky has three "rules" for evolvable systems:

1. Only solutions that produce partial results when partially implemented can succeed. The network is littered with ideas that would
   have worked had everybody adopted them.
2. What is, is wrong. Because evolvable systems have always been
   adapted to earlier conditions and are always being further adapted to
   present conditions, they are always behind the times.
3. Orgel's Rule: "Evolution is cleverer than you are." As with the list of
   the Web's obvious deficiencies above, it is easy to point out what is
   wrong with any evolvable system at any point in its life.

(Shirky 1996)

Both Raymond and Shirky reveal the ideological grounds on which the open-
source movement took off. In fact, in the "epilog" of his essay, Raymond
applauds Netscape's decision in 1998 to give away the source code for
Netscape Communicator (later Navigator and much later Mozilla Firefox).
In 2000, when Raymond wrote the epilog, he described Mozilla as an
"unqualified success." Indeed it was, far beyond even his scope. As of 2010,
Mozilla Firefox is second only to Microsoft's Internet Explorer, and is widely
praised by technologists as being the most stable and secure of all browsers.

Both Shirky and Raymond are identifying, in effect, a new kind of user
and a new system of values or moral economy that is emerging out of the
open-source movement. The user is not simply a consumer but a
"co-developer," who (in theory) can have a direct effect on the software

that he or she is using. As Shirky puts it, open source does not have a "resource horizon" like commercial software. It does not have "some upper boundary of money or programmer time which limits how much can be done on any given project" (Shirky 1999). On the contrary, open source does not operate within the horizon of money or labor time but through what he calls the "interest horizon." "Programmers creating open source software do it because they're interested in it, not because they're paid to do it," as he writes (Shirky 1999).

As the following chapter will show, "the user" and "user-generated content" become important themes in the development of Web 2.0. The open-source movement, we have argued, is where you can find the seeds of Web 2.0. It is where ideas about collaboration and user-generated content—two bedrock principles of Web 2.0—were first articulated. It can be said, then, that the overall "thesis" of this chapter is to argue that the user-centric, collaborative features that have given the phrase "Web 2.0" such purchase can be found in the open-source software movement.

The history of Web 2.0 is a history of the open-source movement.

Notes

1 In fact, as many scholars have noted, various technological advances in the twentieth century, not only the Internet, have had some interaction at its origins with the American military. See De Landa, M., 1991. *War in the Age of Intelligent Machines*, Zone Books.

2 The computer also has an alternative history as "calculating machine." This is traced back to the early nineteenth century, with Charles Babbage's "analytical machine," which used principles of the Jacquard loom.

3 In 1961 Leonard Kleinrock presented the theory of packets to Lawrence Roberts, a colleague of Licklider at MIT, who took over the ARPA office from him.

4 See Han, S., 2007. *Navigating Technomedia: Caught in the Web*, Rowman & Littlefield.

5 The most well-known study of the WELL and MUDs is Rheingold, H., 2000. *The Virtual Community*, MIT Press. Our preference, however, is Turkle, S., 2005. *The Second Self*, MIT Press.

6 The debate around file sharing and other related themes, including intellectual property, have been covered most extensively by legal scholar Lawrence Lessig. See in particular Lessig, L., 2001. *The Future of Ideas*, Random House.

7 "Hacking" is a term that has suffered from much misunderstanding. The image of the hacker engaging in illegal activity is largely a product of proprietary software company PR and Hollywood hyperbole. Raymond uses the term to signify the modification of software's original code or backend. The best analysis

of hacking as practice and culture that we have come across can be found in the work of anthropologist Gabriella Coleman. See Coleman, E.G. & Golub, A., 2008. Hacker Practice: Moral Genres and the Cultural Articulation of Liberalism, *Anthropological Theory*, 8(3), 255–77; and Coleman, G., 2009. Code is Speech: Legal Tinkering, Expertise, and Protest among Free and Open Source Software Developers, *Cultural Anthropology*, 24(3), 420–54.

References

Chapman, C., 2009. The History of the Internet in a Nutshell, *Six Revisions*. Available at: http://sixrevisions.com/resources/the-history-of-the-internet-in-a-nutshell/. [Accessed May 17, 2010.]

Coleman, E.G. & Golub, A., 2008. Hacker Practice: Moral Genres and the Cultural Articulation of Liberalism, *Anthropological Theory*, 8(3), 255–77.

Coleman, G., 2009. Code is Speech: Legal Tinkering, Expertise, and Protest among Free and Open Source Software Developers, *Cultural Anthropology*, 24(3), 420–54.

De Landa, M., 1991. *War in the Age of Intelligent Machines*, Zone Books.

Economist, 2009. The Internet at Forty, *The Economist*. Available at: http://www.economist.com/sciencetechnology/displaystory.cfm?story_id=14391822. [Accessed April 14, 2010.]

Han, S., 2007. *Navigating Technomedia: Caught in the Web*, Rowman & Littlefield.

Lessig, L., 2001. *The Future of Ideas*, Random House.

Lewine, I.B.E., 2007. The Encyclopedist's Lair, *New York Times Magazine*. Available at: http://www.nytimes.com/2007/11/18/magazine/18wwln-domains-t.html. [Accessed May 18, 2010.]

Myers, R., 2010. The GNU Operating System, *GNU Operating System*. Available at: http://www.gnu.org/. [Accessed May 17, 2010.]

Raymond, E.S., 2002. The Cathedral and the Bazaar. Available at: http://www.catb.org/~esr/writings/cathedral-bazaar/cathedral-bazaar/. [Accessed May 19, 2010.]

Rheingold, H., 2000. *The Virtual Community*, MIT Press.

Shirky, C., 1999. The Open Source Interest Horizon, *Clay Shirky's Writings About the Internet*. Available at: http://www.shirky.com/writings/interest.html. [Accessed May 20, 2010.]

——, 1996. In Praise of Evolvable Systems, *Clay Shirky's Writings About the Internet*. Available at: http://www.shirky.com/writings/evolve.html. [Accessed May 19, 2010.]

Stallman, R., 2000. Re: Evaluation of Gcompris. Available at: http://www.gnu.org/encyclopedia/anencyc.txt. [Accessed May 17, 2010.]

Turkle, S., 2005. *The Second Self*, MIT Press.

2

WHAT IS THE "2.0" IN "WEB 2.0"?

According to Dutch net critic Geert Lovink, Web 2.0 was the reincarnation of the World Wide Web in the wake of the dot-com boom and bust. He lays out the landscape of Web 2.0 in the following way:

> Blogs, wikis, and "social networks" such as Friendster, MySpace, Orkut, and Flickr were presented as the next wave of voluntary alliances that users seek online. Virtual communities had become a discredited term, "associated with discredited ideas about cyberspace as an independent polity, and failed dotcom ideas about assembling community in the shadow of a mass-market brand such as forums on the Coca Cola site." Instead, there was talk of swarms, mobs, and crowds. Media had turned social.
>
> *(Lovink 2007, p. ix)*

Although, as we will see in greater detail in the Chapter 5, Lovink is highly critical of Web 2.0, he is right on in his description of what is usually associated with Web 2.0. For him, Web 2.0 figures into his greater periodization of Internet culture. The first period of the Internet was the "scientific, precommercial, text-only period before the Web." The next step was the "the euphoric, speculative, period in which the Internet opened up for general audience." The current period, "the post-dot-com crash/post-9/11 period . . . is now coming to a close with the Web 2.0 mini-bubble." Clearly, Lovink is unsympathetic to the term "Web 2.0" and sees it as a mainly rhetorical tool to drum up hype for Web 2.0 business.

Web 1.0 vs. Web 2.0: what's the difference?

As previously stated, Tim O'Reilly first used the term "Web 2.0" with the announcement of his Web 2.0 Conference in October 2004. The 2.0, as O'Reilly has explained, was a way to designate that, in the wake of the dot-com bust in 2001, the Web had not gone away, but had, in fact, been reborn. In a widely circulated article called "What is Web 2.0: Design Patterns and Business Models for the Next Generation of Software," O'Reilly lays out the key differences between Web 1.0 and 2.0. He includes a rather helpful table to highlight them.

Although clearly revealing the corporate (business-minded) orientation of O'Reilly, the list does a good enough job at pointing out the key differences between the two. For instance, we see that Britannica Online is in the Web 1.0 column, while Wikipedia is in the Web 2.0 column. This

TABLE 2.1 Key differences between Web 1.0 and 2.0

Web 1.0	Web 2.0
DoubleClick	Google AdSense
Ofoto	Flickr
Akamai	BitTorrent
mp3.com	Napster
Britannica Online	Wikipedia
personal websites	blogging
evite	upcoming.org and EVDB
domain name speculation	search engine optimization
page views	cost per click
screen scraping	web services
publishing	participation
content management systems	wikis
directories (taxonomy)	tagging ("folksonomy")
Stickiness	syndication

distinction, as already detailed in the previous chapter, is clear. Britannica Online is simply the traditional encyclopedia going from one medium (the printed word) to the Web. Although Britannica Online undoubtedly offers features that a shelfworth of volumes could not, such as a keyword search and hyperlinks to related articles, the content is still written, maintained, and edited by a select group of experts hired by the Encyclopædia Britannica, Inc. Along with this illustration are several key principles of Web 2.0:

1. The Web as platform.
2. Harnessing collective intelligence.
3. Data are the next Intel Inside.
4. Lightweight programming models.
5. End of software release cycle.
6. Software above the level of a single device.
7. Rich user experience.

(1) The first is that the Web is a platform. A platform facilitates. It allows others to interact with it and on it. This, as O'Reilly rightly points out, is not something that is new with the onset of Web 2.0. In fact, this was some part of the impetus behind Web 1.0. Indeed, Web 2.0 is not so much a hard break from its predecessor but rather "a fuller realization of the true potential of the Web platform". Web 2.0, therefore, is not a bounded entity but a "set of principles and practices that tie together a veritable solar system of sites." To put this in concrete terms, we can think of Web 2.0 as populated mostly by Web services *not* software. A company that operates under this service logic is Google. Its flagship "product," the search, is a Web application. O'Reilly describes it thusly:

> None of the trappings of the old software industry are [sic] present. No scheduled software release, just continuous improvement. No licensing or sale, just usage. No porting to different platforms so that customers can run the software on their own equipment . . .

Google has successively become the medium itself for many forms of communication with its suite of Web applications, which include Gmail, Google Reader, Google Wave and Google Docs. None of these is in any way a "standalone" application, that is, a program that you install onto your computer (although some of them *do* have that feature). Primarily, these Web applications are used *on* the Web, through users' Web browsers.

(2) Additionally, O'Reilly suggests that another key principle is the harnessing of "collective intelligence," a phrase that he adopts from the French media theorist Pierre Levy. Levy understands the term as "the enhancement, optimal use, and fusion of skill, imagination, and intellectual energy, regardless of their qualitative diversity." In other words, contemporary media technologies have created new conditions for knowledge:

> Knowledge is structured through a network of cross-references, possibly already inhabited by hypertext. Here the concept, abstraction, and system serve to condense memory and ensure the intellectual control that the inflation of knowledge already endangers.
>
> *(Levy 2001, p.144)*

Practical examples of the harnessing of collective intelligence on the Web consist of Web services taking in user data in order to improve themselves. This is what O'Reilly calls the "architecture of participation" (O'Reilly 2005). Arguing against what he believes to be overemphasis on ideologies of altruism or volunteerism in Web 2.0 (for instance, in the writings of Stallman, Raymond, and Shirky summarized in the previous chapter), O'Reilly suggests that it is not the subject intent of the users but the architecture of the Web that facilitates "users pursuing their own 'selfish' interests" that "build collective value as an automatic byproduct" (O'Reilly 2005). One can see this also in the architecture of blogs. Each post usually has a comments section. Discussion is built in. It is this principle that so many of the buzz terms surrounding Web 2.0 reflect—"wisdom of crowds" and "global brain."

(3) O'Reilly also suggests that data become important in a different way with Web 2.0. As he suggests, they become akin to the semiconductor company Intel, whose processors are inside the majority of computers today, no matter the operating system—Windows, Mac, or otherwise. Similarly, control over databases is no longer as important as obtaining licenses for data and providing a slick software application for those data. An example of this is news aggregation for which there are so many Web applications—Yahoo! News and Google News are just two among many.

They both cull data from a variety of sources, ranging from services like Associated Press and Reuters as well as newspapers such as the *Washington Post* and the *Los Angeles Times* to blogs. The reason why users prefer one over the other, or why one does better than the other, is not because of exclusive access or control to the data (the news, in this instance) but through presentation. One could think about this principle as the triumph of form over content.

(4) In turn, programming for a variety of Web services has become far more lightweight. It allows for more "hackability" and, most importantly for Web 2.0, reuse. An instance of this is the widespread use of RSS (real simple syndication) that allows for services to simply push data out and not control what happens to them afterwards. This is exactly the kind of thing that occurred with the social networking site MySpace, whose source code, while not completely open, was open enough for users to modify the look of their individual pages. Now, MySpace is full of customized pages.

(5) If, indeed, Web applications are receiving constant feedback from their users, whom they treat as co-developers, then there is no longer the need for the traditional cycle of software releases. In the age of Web 2.0, this has been released mostly by software updates, *not* releases—the key difference being that updates do not have to be purchased as releases do. The most visible vestiges of the release cycle are in the realm of operating systems for both Macs and Windows, which still have scheduled releases. What has replaced this is a more immediate debugging and improvement experience. Web applications are often updated in order for them to operate smoothly. Daily operation trumps new releases.

(6) In the era of Web services, no longer desktop applications, software must necessarily rise above the level of a single device. In other words, if an application is not multi-platform, it is surely not going to succeed. Many Web applications such as Twitter have open API (application programming interface) whereby software developers are able to create client programs for use on various devices such as mobile phones.

(7) Lastly, Web 2.0 has a distinct user experience, which O'Reilly describes as "rich." Web services mirror applications in the "richness" of their user experience. In other words, when one is using an application on the Web such as Google Maps, there is no detectable dropoff in the experience. "Web developers are finally able to build Web applications as rich as local-PC based applications" (O'Reilly 2005).

There is no doubt that these principles are, in fact, simplistic generalizations made by O'Reilly, who has a clear interest in making money out of the "achievement" of Web 2.0. Furthermore, we must acknowledge the gap between the "phenomena" of Web 2.0 and the ideals laid out by O'Reilly. To reconcile the phenomena and the ideal of Web 2.0, let us now move on to some of the uses and practices of Web 2.0, looking specifically at blogging.

Blogging

Blogging is perhaps the most recognized of the Web 2.0 phenomena, and for several reasons. It has somehow exhibited lasting power due to a number of different factors, the most identifiable being that blogging has become widespread to the point that nearly all corporations, individuals, and religious and education institutions have a blog. Blogs in the era of Web 2.0 have broken out of their geeky shell.

But what exactly is a blog?

> A blog is commonly defined as a frequently updated Web-based chronological publication, a log of personal thoughts and Web links, a mixture of comments on what is happening on the Web and the world out there. The blog allows for the easy creation of new pages: text and pictures are entered into an online template within the Web browser (usually tagged by title, category, and the body of the article) and this data is then submitted. Automated templates take care of adding the article to the home page, creating the new full article page (called a permalink), and adding the article to the appropriate date- or category-based archive. Because of the tags that the author puts into each posting, blogs let us filter by date, category, author or other attributes. It (usually) allows the administrator to invite and add other authors, whose permissions and access are easily managed.
>
> *(Lovink 2007, p.3)*

When "blog" first emerged as a term, it was associated with adolescents who spent too much time in front of the computer and had begun to keep a public journal. One of the earliest of the websites that hosted blogs was called "LiveJournal," which was started in 1999, years before the idea for Web 2.0 had even been thought of.

Not all blogs are equal, however. There exists, indeed, a hierarchy of blogs, ever since their proliferation started. Today, the most recognized blogs are news blogs—*Huffington Post* being the most prominent. But the point is not that there is a hierarchy or an influence differential within the blogosphere but that blogs are no longer subversive or subcultural. The bastions of journalistic prestige in the United States, *The New Yorker* and *The Atlantic*, have (very good, might we just add) blogs. Why blogs have become so popular is that they offer a less formal and shorter venue for writers to report in, opine, or just rant. Lastly, they allow for more *frequent* updates than traditional paper-based journalism.

In effect, news blogs signal the "de-expertization" of journalism. Jay Rosen, a prominent news critic and journalism professor, in a widely read op-ed in the *Washington Post* criticizes the rather late response of major news organizations in thinking about the World Wide Web. They were stuck in a "news-as-lecture" mode while the future was pointing towards a "news-as-conversation" mode (Rosen 2006). The significance of this was that, as Rosen argues, the gates had been bust open. In other words, news media, like the *Washington Post*, had largely been "gated," that is, closed off from the audience. Between journalist and non-journalist was not only educational accreditation but also the means and resources by which to distribute information. This all changed with the World Wide Web and blogging. As Rosen says, a new balance of power was struck between producer and consumers:

> The basic idea of what defines a news "consumer" morphs when consumers gain access to producers' tools, and can float between being a reader and an editor. In a speech to BBC staff on April 25, 2006, the network's director-general, Mark Thompson, said users with expanded choices demand more from big brands. New media, he said, "empowers those audiences, transfers control from us to them, lets them consume what they want, when they want, lets them create content, lets them participate."
>
> *(Rosen 2006)*

Rosen's description here is important as it provides for us the kind of shift that news organizations have attempted in recent years. For an illustration, let us turn to *The Atlantic*. Its online operation is certainly the most robust of the magazines that are online, rivaling even the likes of those such as Salon, which operates strictly online. What sets *The Atlantic* apart is that it has full-time, paid bloggers, who are prominent writers. This group includes (or has included) the likes of Andrew Sullivan, Ta-Nehisi Coates, and Matthew Yglesias. In addition, *The Atlantic* also launched *The Atlantic Wire*, a self-described "one-stop portal for opinion news," aggregating the top news stories, political commentators, and columnists—whom it calls "opinion-makers" (Carlson 2009). Both the bloggers at *The Atlantic* and its sister site post not only regularly but frequently. Sullivan and Coates both post several times a day. Most posts consist of links to other news or opinion sources with some commentary. This aggregative aspect of blogging fits right in with the "Web as platform" ethic of Web 2.0.

The posts serve as points of discussion throughout the day. The structure of the blog mirrors what O'Reilly calls the "architecture of participation." Every post necessarily contains a comments section that allows visitors to leave comments. It is here where the bloggers interact with their audience. Although by now the very fact of interactivity is utterly mundane, this kind of contact between writer and audience is unprecedented. Further, comments sections are where many relationships are formed. There are, at times, vigorous yet substantive discussions that occur in comments sections. (This fact does not emerge with the rise of blogging. To the contrary, the success of blogging has come in large part due to the comments sections' similarity to the BBS (discussion board) and email listserv of yester-Web.)

The person who has most forcefully challenged this view of blogging has been Geert Lovink. In a widely circulated essay called "Blogging, the Nihilist Impulse," he suggests that a narrative similar to Rosen's has overrun the discourse around the phenomena of blogging. It too easily gives credence to O'Reilly's corpo-ideology of Web 2.0. Lovink goes after the idea that Rosen in particular adheres to, which is that blogging (and Web 2.0 more generally) is one rung in the ladder of the progressive democratization of American media. On top of the fact that much of the blogosphere is right leaning, as Lovink points out, blogging is reflective of pervasive cynicism in the post-9/11 Zeitgeist. He calls this "Internet reason."

By "Internet reason," Lovink is detailing what he believes to be the rather unserious, and conservative, nature of Web 2.0, in particular the blogosphere. (We will consider Lovink's larger criticisms of Web 2.0 in the final chapter alongside another Web 2.0 critic, Nicholas Carr.) Blogs, according to him, are a reduced form of writing. While emails and, by extension, the listserv culture fall within the tradition of letter writing, blog posts, due to their length (or lack thereof) and their rather outward looking nature (in that blog posts usually revolve around link sharing), resemble "zippy public relations techniques" (Lovink 2007, p.4). They also act very much *within* mainstream media, in spite of the way in which they are portrayed as somehow threatening large news corporations. Drawing from Axel Bruns, Lovink labels blogs as "gatewatchers." They monitor the news media and "comment on the choices of those who control the news gates" (Lovink 2007, p.5):

> To blog a news report doesn't mean that the blogger sits down and thoroughly analyzes the discourse and circumstances, let alone checks the facts. To blog merely means to quickly point to news facts through a link and a few sentences that explain why the blogger found this or that factoid interesting or remarkable or is in disagreement with it.
>
> Blog entries are often hastily written personal musings, sculptured around a link or event. In most cases, bloggers simply do not have the time, skills, and the financial means to do proper research. There are collective research blogs, working on specific topics, but these are rare. *What ordinary blogs create is a dense cloud of impressions around a topic.* Blogs will tell you if your audience is still awake and receptive. Blogs test. In that sense, we could also say that blogs are the outsourced, privatized test beds, or rather the unit tests of the big media.
>
> *(Lovink 2007, p.7)*

What he objects to is the seemingly unserious nature of the enterprise of blogging. It does more to obfuscate news than it does to clarify it. On a related point, he notes that blogging is rather mundane. There is very little room for analysis. Blogging seems to be, in Lovink's mind, sharing for the sake of sharing. Although we do not totally agree with the conclusions that Lovink reaches with regard to blogging and sharing, his point is nonetheless an important one if one wishes to understand the user culture of

Web 2.0. A sticking point for Lovink is what he views to be the obligation to share. This he believes to be reflective of a "pastoral power."[1]

But, by way of contrast, Lovink does acknowledge that blogging contains a nihilist impulse. For him then, the irony of "content production," which has been a recent slogan of sorts, is that there is evidence, especially in light of the rise of the blogosphere, that there is a declining "belief in the message," as he calls it (Lovink 2007, p.17). Blogs, he explains, are not aiming at knowledge. Thus, he makes a distinction between nihilism and cynicism: "Whereas cynicism refers to knowledge, nihilism relates to existence and nothingness" (Lovink 2007, p.16):

> Often blogs unveil doubts and insecurity about what to feel, what to think, believe, and like. They carefully compare magazines and review traffic signs, nightclubs, and t-shirts. This stylized uncertainty circles around the general assumption that blogs ought to be biographical while simultaneously reporting about the world outside . . . What blogs play with is the emotional register, varying from hate to boredom, passionate engagement, sexual outrage, and back to everyday boredom.
>
> *(Lovink 2007)*

As Lovink goes on to argue, blogs are representative of the original meaning of nihilism—"creative destruction," not really absence of meaning. Bloggers are "nothingists" in that they actively undermine the centralized meaning-production of mainstream news media. The "gatewatching" function of the blogosphere is reflective of what I have elsewhere symptomized as a shift in knowledge itself towards what I call "unreason."[2]

Further, this "gatewatching" has arguably proliferated to the point where Lovink's own statements regarding the general conservatism of the blogosphere can be refuted. According to Michael Massing, the conservative hegemony of the blogosphere no longer exists as it used to in 2005. With websites such as Talking Points Memo, a left-leaning website that gained notoriety (and a George Polk Award) for uncovering the questionable firing of US attorneys during the Bush administration, Massing argues that in the blogosphere "today, the liberal left is ascendant (with energy among conservatives channeled instead into talk radio)" (Massing 2009).

We can say that, for Lovink, blogging embodies a contradiction. On the one hand, it provides a counterpoint to the gatekeepers of information, the mainstream media. On the other, it can create an echo chamber of discrete messages that do not mount to a critique or even analysis. Blogging, however, does not encapsulate the *ethos* of Web 2.0 as embodied in O'Reilly's principles. Let us turn briefly to look at one Web service that has become a "success story," if you will, of user culture—Flickr, a photo-sharing website and social network.

Flickr

Flickr is a photo-sharing website and social network that was started by Caterina Fake and Stewart Butterfield in 2004. By 2005, while it was still in beta, Flickr had close to 250,000 members and was growing 5–10 percent a week, with members uploading 60,000 photos a day. In 2007 Flickr had its 2 billionth image uploaded, averaging 3–5 million photos on its site daily (Arrington 2007). Flickr's success is attributable to a few aspects of the technological conditions on top of which Web 2.0 sits, which we outlined briefly in the Introduction. For one, Flickr relies on the wide availability of digital cameras, either in standalone form or on mobile devices. Additionally, Flickr relies on the variety of means whereby one can upload and view photos. To upload photos, one can go to Flickr.com or the Flickr Uploader, a desktop application made by Flickr for Mac and Windows operating systems. There is also a variety of third-party upload tools for photo management software such as Apple's iPhoto. To view images, you can obviously go to Flickr. com. But additionally, you can use RSS feeds to particular users, groups or tags, HTML embed codes to blogs, and a variety of other methods, including screensavers, which had been able to be developed by users due to the open accessibility of Flickr's API (application programming interface). Other applications are compiled in Flickr's "App Garden."

Flickr has received a lot of attention for "tagging," its inventive means of organizing and categorizing photos. For each photo or set of photos uploaded, the user is prompted to add keywords, as many as he or she wants, to describe the photo. These tags then make up the organizational infrastructure whereby users can share their photos. For instance, if you type in "Seoul" in the search on Flickr.com, you get over 780,000 photos that are tagged by other users with "Seoul."

Fake, one of its founders, explained to the *Guardian* that the idea for tagging came from del.icio.us, the social bookmarking site that allowed users to store bookmarks online and therefore access them from any computer with Internet access. As she says, "it was the first site to really show what could happen when users were allowed to create tags to organize information online themselves then share it with others" (McClellan 2005). Further, one can tag others' photos in addition to being able to leave notes. This principle of self-organization has spun off some amazing creative "Flickr fads," user-generated tags that act as a trope, such as "squared circle." If you search that tag, you will find thousands of photos of a circle in a square.

This mode of user-generated data organization has largely been understood through a framework called "folksonomy," a term coined by Thomas Vander Wal on a listserv of information architects to describe "user-created bottom-up categorical structure development" (Vander Wal 2007). As can be deduced from the words from which "folksonomy" draw, "folks" and "taxonomy," Vander Wal suggests that it is primarily a form of classification practiced by everyday people; more specifically, one whereby the *consumer*, in addition to the producer of the information, is allowed to categorize. It is a means of organizing it for future retrieval. The key is that tagging, as Vander Wal formulates it, is first and foremost for the person consuming the data. It is from this "personal" value that greater categorical value is then created:

> The value in this external tagging is derived from people using their own vocabulary and adding explicit meaning, which may come from inferred understanding of the information/object. People are not so much categorizing, as providing a means to connect items (placing hooks) to provide their meaning in their own understanding.
>
> *(Vander Wal 2007)*

In 2005 the *New York Times* gave this illustration to explain how this works:

> A folksonomy begins with tagging. On the Web site Flickr, for example, users post their photos and label them with descriptive words. You might tag the picture of your cat, "cat," "Sparky" and "living room." Then you'll be able to retrieve that photo when

you're searching for the cute shot of Sparky lounging on the couch. If you open your photos and tags to others, as many Flickr devotees do, other people can examine and label your photos. A furniture aficionado might add the tag "Mitchell Gold sofa," which means that he and others looking for images of this particular kind of couch could find your photo . . . [T]he cumulative force of all the individual tags can produce a bottom-up, self-organized system for classifying mountains of digital material.

(Pink 2005)

While for Vander Wal, the value of Flickr is the "folksonomic" practices that engender what Tim O'Reilly, drawing from Pierre Levy, speaks of as "collective intelligence," others viewed the *sharing* nature of Flickr to be most important.

Due to its enormity (both in membership and in number of uploaded photos) and its emphasis on openness (thanks in large part to its use of the Creative Commons license), Flickr is not only a social network and photo-sharing site, but also a resource. It has become one of the major troves of photographic images that bloggers and other new media writers draw from in order to add images to blog posts and the like. According to Fake, 80 percent of the photos on Flickr are public (Torrone 2004), thus, up for the taking and reusing by others as long as the photographer is attributed.

Lawrence Lessig views this ethos in terms of a new cultural formation, which he calls "RW" or read-writable. He adopts RW from the language of computer file extensions. RO (read-only) files have their settings so that one could only read the information contained therein as determined by the original writer. RW allows for additions from others. RW culture is rooted in the "remix," which Lessig identifies as the "right to quote" (Lessig 2008, p.56). An example that Lessig gives of an "offline" RW culture is writing. As he says:

We understand quoting is an essential part of . . . writing. It should be impossible to construct and support that practice if permission were required every time a quote was made. The freedom to quote, and to build upon, the words of others is taken for granted by everyone who writes.

(Lessig 2008, p.53)

Lessig views tagging within this framework. Tagging is like "writing" in that it is a creative, democratic practice that when enough people participate, you create what he calls a "layer of meaning," similar to what Michel Foucault once called a "discursive formation." For Lessig, tagging is just as creative and significant as the original content and "more useful and significant" are more of them are created. "As the reader 'writes' with tags ... the importance of the original writing changes" (Lessig 2008, p.60). What is crucial about tagging is that this layer of discourse is determined not by any commercial entities but by other users/consumers. The folksonomic layer is a semi-autonomous sphere of creativity based on not on profit first and foremost but rather an "economy of reputation." According to Lessig, the procurement of RW culture is crucial for democracy. Hence, he suggests that the remix is a "critical expression of creative freedom that in a broad range of contexts, no free society should restrict" (Lessig 2008, p.56).

Collectivism

Recently, a discussion about the politics of social media has emerged in light of Web 2.0 about the very issue that Lessig raises with "remix," sparked by an article written by Kevin Kelly, founding editor of *Wired* magazine, called "The New Socialism: Global Collectivist Society is Coming Online" (Kelly 2009). Here, Kelly argues that Web 2.0 and its folksonomic practices are a new cultural movement (Kelly 2009). Prior to Kelly's article, which prompted a response by Lessig (which we will discuss shortly), Clay Shirky had noted that all "social software is political science in executable form" (Shirky 2003). Although Shirky may be engaging in a degree of hyperbole, what he means by this is that any given social system (including software and websites) necessarily contains rules that administer the relationship between groups and individuals. They encourage some types of action and discourage others. This, for him, determines the "politics" of the social software itself. Hence, it is unsurprising that Kelly, similarly disposed to overstatement, suggested that the "frantic global rush to connect everyone to everyone, all the time," as embodied in Wikipedia, Flickr, and Twitter, "is quietly giving rise to a revised version of socialism" (Kelly 2009).

Kelly argues this by highlighting what he calls the "communal aspects of digital culture," the "wikiness at large" that is now virtually hegemonic on the Web. We have explained some of these practices in some detail already. First, he attempts to disambiguate the term "socialism" by suggesting that "digital socialism" is not "your grandfather's socialism" that is organized around the state. He states that he uses socialism because, cultural baggage notwithstanding, it is the best term to describe what he is getting at: "It is the best word to indicate a range of technologies that rely for their power on social interactions" (Kelly 2009).

It is a socialism that operates in the realm of culture and economics.

In turn, this form of socialism is necessarily decentralized. Just as it differs from old-school socialism due to its functioning outside the realm of government, digital socialism is rooted in the Internet, which disrespects borders left and right. As Kelly wonderfully describes it:

> Instead of gathering on collective farms, we gather in collective worlds. Instead of state factories, we have desktop factories connected to virtual co-ops. Instead of sharing drill bits, picks, and shovels, we share apps, scripts, and APIs. Instead of faceless polit-buros, we have faceless meritocracies, where the only thing that matters is getting things done. Instead of national production, we have peer production. Instead of government rations and subsidies, we have a bounty of free goods.
>
> *(Kelly 2009)*[3]

In spite of his overuse of the word socialism, what Kelly really means to drive home is the spirit of collectivism that has emerged in social media. Collectivism encompasses for him a fundamentally new mode of production. "The aim of a collective," as he writes:

> . . . is to engineer a system where self-directed peers take responsibility for critical processes and where difficult decisions, such as sorting out priorities, are decided by all participants.
>
> *(Kelly 2009)*

It is different, Kelly claims, than that of contemporary capitalism because it is rooted on a different set of priorities. Collectivism, while trying to avoid hierarchy, is more interested in maximizing individual autonomy and the power of people working together by engineering "a system where self-directed peers take responsibility for critical processes and where difficult decisions, such as sorting priorities, are decided by all participants" (Kelly 2009). However, in many instances, this may mean that, while trying to achieve these goals, some endeavors that express the spirit of collectivism most boldly indeed have traces of hierarchy, which Kelly calls "governing kernel," in endeavors such as Wikipedia, Linux, and OpenOffice (an open-source, non-proprietary alternative to the Microsoft Office suite). While many are able to contribute to these efforts, there are, for many of them, a top layer of editors who sift through all the contributions. For Kelly, this does not necessarily undermine the collectivist impulse as long as the barriers of entry are low.

In fact, Kelly himself betrays the radical edge of any proposal to take "socialism" seriously in the twenty-first century United States by calling "digital socialism" a "third way," evoking the neoliberal regime of the Clinton and Blair administrations. He goes on to point out the fact that the new social production of the Web has eclipsed what the open-source movement had already shown: people are willing to work, share, and use things for free not only because they are genuinely interested in them (open source) but also because they like to be part of something larger than their individual existences.

But what Kelly does not take into consideration is how the social data that users' sharing and liking provides profit for the Web services but do not trickle down to the users themselves. Take, for instance, Facebook, which in February 2009 announced that it would experiment with "engagement ads" (Davis 2009), as a means by which corporations could attempt market research. As the *Telegraph* reported at the time:

> Companies will be able to pose questions to specially selected members based on such intimate details as whether they are single or married and even whether they are gay or straight.
>
> *(Neate & Mason 2009)*

This would extend to Facebook's more recent feature of being able to "like" something that someone has posted on their wall or someone else's wall.

This could then be sold to corporations as a means to mine data about what products, music, and other commodities are most "liked" by Facebook users. In effect, it would be a database of taste.

What Kelly seems to miss is the arguably exploitative profit-making aspects of the model that he heralds as "socialist." Indeed, the question that one must ask is: is there a similar production and extraction of value in what various scholars, including Michael Hardt and Antonio Negri, refer to as the "new economy," whereby the location of value production shifts from labor time?[4] Are the data-mining practices of Facebook, among other Web services, exploitation, albeit a much softer kind? Is what Kelly is describing perhaps not as radical as he deems it?

This is the moderate position of Lawrence Lessig, who not only takes exception to Kelly's use of the term "socialism," but also to what he perceives to be the mischaracterization of Web 2.0 or "sharing economy" as socialist. While acknowledging that Kelly and he are largely in agreement about the practices and empirical descriptions of the current trends in Web 2.0, Lessig uses "hybrid economy" instead. A hybrid economy is, he notes, "either a commercial entity that aims to leverage value from a sharing economy, or it is a sharing economy that builds a commercial entity to better support its sharing aims" (Lessig 2008, p.177). This means that companies are not sacrificing their bottom lines. They are, as Lessig rather comically notes, not "[behaving] like Gandhi."

> The Facebooks and Twitters and Flickrs and Yelps! are not entities engaged in a global urge to hug. They are companies that promise investors a huge return from their very risky investment. To do that, of course, they need to behave differently from the dominant mode of, say, Hollywood lawyers ... their mission ... is (however much "change the world" or "don't be evil" is in the plan) to make money.
>
> *(Lessig 2009)*

Conclusion

Whether Kelly or Lessig agree on the merits of labeling the collection of practices known as Web 2.0 socialism or not, it is undoubtedly the case that something new is here. Although it may be an oversimplification of the various trends and practices that fall under its heading, Web 2.0 is rooted in what we have called in this chapter "user culture." Taking from the ethic of "hacking" in the open-source movement, Web 2.0 has, in some ways, broadened what was only available to a specialized community of hackers. Indeed, this thread of allowing the users of the particular software product to have a say in it. This upturns the traditional dichotomy between "producer" and "consumer," in turn, upturning the inherent power relations between the two:

> The increased importance of the user resulted in a change in what we understand to be "economy."

Let us now to turn to some of the ways in which social formations have changed with Web 2.0.

Notes

1 Beginning with the last volume of his *History of Sexuality*, Foucault began to investigate in great detail different regimes of power in European history. In particular, he was interested in modes of self-discipline. That is, he was asking when the self became an object for a moral project.
2 For a more detailed analysis of the shift in knowledge that we are talking about, see Han, S., 2007. *Navigating Technomedia: Caught in the Web*, Rowman & Littlefield (particularly Chapter 2).
3 To make things even clearer, he offers up this graphic: http://www.wired.com/culture/culturereviews/magazine/17-06/nep_newsocialism/
4 See Hardt, M., 1999. Affective Labor, *Boundary 2*, 89–100; see also Hardt, M. & Negri, A., 2001. *Empire*, Harvard University Press.

References

Facebook | Pages. Available at: http://www.facebook.com/advertising/?pages. [Accessed June 18, 2010.]

Arrington, M., 2007. 2 Billion Photos On Flickr, *TechCrunch*. Available at: http://techcrunch.com/2007/11/13/2-billion-photos-on-flickr/. [Accessed May 29, 2010.]

Carlson, B., 2009. About Us | The Atlantic Wire, *The Atlantic*. Available at: http://www.theatlanticwire.com/opinions/view/opinion/About-Us-1003. [Accessed May 25, 2010.]

Davis, L., 2009. Facebook Plans to Make Money by Selling Your Data, *Read Write Web*. Available at: http://www.readwriteweb.com/archives/facebook_sells_your_data.php. [Accessed June 7, 2010.]

Dibbell, J., 2005. Pic Your Friends, *The Village Voice*. Available at: http://www.villagevoice.com/2005/screens/pic-your-friends/. [Accessed May 28, 2010.]

Han, S., 2007. *Navigating Technomedia: Caught in the Web*, Rowman & Littlefield.

Hardt, M., 1999. Affective Labor, *Boundary 2*, 89–100.

Hardt, M. & Negri, A., 2001. *Empire*, Harvard University Press.

Kelly, K., 2009. The New Socialism: Global Collectivist Society Is Coming Online. *Wired*, 17(06). Available at: http://www.wired.com/culture/culturereviews/magazine/17-06/nep_newsocialism. [Accessed June 5, 2010.]

Lessig, L., 2009. On "Socialism": Round II (Lessig Blog), *Lessig*. Available at: http://www.lessig.org/blog/2009/05/on_socialism_round_ii.html. [Accessed June 8, 2010.]

—— , 2008. *Remix: Making Art and Commerce Thrive in the Hybrid Economy*, Penguin.

Levy, P., 2001. *Cyberculture* 1st edn, University of Minnesota Press.

—— , 1997. *Collective Intelligence* 1st edn, Basic Books.

Lovink, G., 2007. *Zero Comments: Blogging and Critical Internet Culture* 1st edn, Routledge.

Massing, M., 2009. The News About the Internet, *New York Review of Books* (13 August 2009). Available at: http://www.nybooks.com/articles/archives/2009/aug/13/the-news-about-the-internet/. [Accessed June 1, 2010.]

McClellan, J., 2005. Tag Team, *Guardian*. Available at: http://www.guardian.co.uk/technology/2005/feb/03/onlinesupplement2. [Accessed May 28, 2010.]

Neate, R. & Mason, R., 2009. Networking Site Cashes in on Friends, *Telegraph.co.uk*. Available at: http://www.telegraph.co.uk/finance/newsbysector/mediatech-nologyandtelecoms/4413483/Networking-site-cashes-in-on-friends.html. [Accessed June 7, 2010.]

O'Reilly, T., 2005. What is Web 2.0: Design Patterns and Business Models for the Next Generation of Software, *O'Reilly Media*. Available at: http://oreilly.com/web2/archive/what-is-web-20.html. [Accessed May 21, 2010.]

Odlyzko, A., 2001. Content is not King, *First Monday*, 6(2). Available at: http://firstmonday.org/htbin/cgiwrap/bin/ojs/index.php/fm/article/viewArticle/833/742. [Accessed June 2, 2010.]

Pink, D.H., 2005. Folksonomy, *New York Times*. Available at: http://www.nytimes.com/2005/12/11/magazine/11ideas1-21.html?_r=1. [Accessed May 28, 2010.]

Rosen, J., 2006. Web Users Open the Gates, *Washington Post*. Available at: http://www.washingtonpost.com/wp-dyn/content/article/2006/06/18/AR2006061800618.html. [Accessed May 25, 2010.]

Shirky, C., 2003. Social Software and the Politics of Groups, *Clay Shirky's Writings About the Internet*. Available at: http://www.shirky.com/writings/group_politics.html. [Accessed June 5, 2010.]

Torrone, P., 2004. Interview with Caterina Fake from Flickr, *Engadget*. Available at: http://www.engadget.com/2004/12/03/interview-with-caterina-fake-from-flickr/. [Accessed May 29, 2010.]

Vander Wal, T., 2007. Folksonomy: Vanderwal.net, *Vanderwal.net*. Available at: http://www.vanderwal.net/folksonomy.html. [Accessed May 30, 2010.]

3

NEW FORMATIONS

The social ambiance of Web 2.0

One of the most frequently discussed aspects of Web 2.0 has been the emergence of new social formations, in particular, social networks. Today, the term "social networks" usually refer to sites such as Facebook and MySpace that are meant to connect people with one another along various lines but usually interests (in music, books, television, etc.) and location. (There are, however, other instances to which we wish to extend the notion of social networks, which we discuss later.) In this chapter, we look at social networks in great detail.

We first consider the history of social networks, using the work of social media researcher danah boyd (she likes her name to be spelled with lowercase letters, just in case you were wondering). We do so to get a better understanding of what exactly social networks are and what exactly they do, since the term has, in the era of Web 2.0, been so often used and misused. We then consider what technology writer Clive Thompson calls "social proprioception" to describe the new wave of social media practices, especially as it relates to the increased popularity of microblogging via Twitter, as a way to understand the emergent social formations of Web 2.0. We will draw from Thompson's work to amplify the way in which sociality can be "felt" in this regard. Lastly, we will discuss the status of "community," an analytic that, we argue, has been overly influential in the way social formations on the World Wide Web are understood.

Social networks

Before the term was used to describe a certain type of website, "social network" was used by some sociologists who were engaged in a particular subfield called "social network analysis," which looks at social organization through network theory terminology, to describe specific group formations. One of the key terms in social network analysis is "weak ties," which describes loose and not-so-entrenched relationships between people. A weak tie would be, for instance, an acquaintance from church. Although by no means someone you would call a friend, this person is someone you see with a degree of regularity. This "church friend" may, however, help you know about a job that she has heard about. The significance of weak ties has been most famously expressed in sociologist Mark Grannovetter's 1973 "The Strength of Weak Ties." In the late 1990s and early 2000s, when Web-based services oriented around the creation of profiles first emerged, they began to be described as "social networks" (a rare occasion whereby sociological terms were appropriated in public discourse, a feat that had not really occurred on this scale since Robert Merton's "self-fulfilling prophesy" took on widespread popularity).

One of the most well-respected researchers on social media is danah boyd. She, along with Nicole Ellison, has provided one of the best overviews and histories of social network sites. A fundamental premise of their overview is the distinction between social *network* sites and social *networking* sites. As they write:

> We chose not to employ the term "networking" for two reasons: emphasis and scope. "Networking" emphasizes relationship initiation, often between strangers. While networking is possible on these sites, it is not the primary practice on many of them, nor is it what differentiates them from other forms of computer-mediated communication (CMC).
> *(boyd & Ellison 2007, p. 2)*

Throughout their overview, boyd and Ellison insist that most interactions on social network sites occur between people who are not complete strangers. (We will return to this point in a moment.) Indeed, this fact in itself is something to note.

Why?

The first wave of research on online "communities" such as MUDs and BBSs focused narrowly on identity formation. Authors such as Howard Rheingold, whose book *The Virtual Community* was one of the earliest studies of the Internet, and Sherry Turkle, in her *Life on the Screen*, studied the otherworldly nature of online interactions. This included interesting practices of gender bending and role playing on various online MUDs, discussion forums, and chat rooms. A lot of this research suggested that online interactions were mainly facilitating connections between complete strangers. Hence, the consensus was that identity play would be prominent in such a context, since no one you know IRL (in real life) would be able to "out" you. This, however, changed with the emergence of the World Wide Web and Web-based social networks.

Social network sites today are less defined by the kinds of intense identity play characteristic of MUDs but more so by what boyd calls "impression management," a term she adopts from sociologist Erving Goffman. She and Ellison argue that this is the case because of the profile-centric nature of contemporary social network sites. Thus their definition of social network sites has three profile-oriented aspects. Social network sites allow individuals to:

(1) construct a public or semi-public profile within a bounded system
(2) articulate a list of other users with whom they share a connection
(3) view and traverse their list of connections and those made by others within the system.

These three aspects already put in relief the differences between the first generation of Internet social spaces and the more recent ones such as social network sites.

Ellison and boyd trace the beginnings of social network sites with the launch of SixDegrees.com in 1997. The basic components of what they define as social network sites (discussed in greater detail later) can be found there. SixDegrees featured profiles, a list of "friends," and the ability to browse these "friends" lists. It must be understood that by no means did SixDegrees create these features. Contact lists, for instance, had been around since the days of instant messaging. Profiles had been around since MUDs and forums and were the basis for online dating sites. What SixDegrees did was to bring these features together and make browsing friends of friends possible. While SixDegrees never took off in the way that subsequent social networks later would, in the period of 1997–2001, these basic features that they had introduced had begun to be picked up by other websites, especially ethnic-affinity sites such as AsianAvenue, BlackPlanet, and MiGente, which were for more content-oriented prior to their becoming-social.

When Friendster.com launched in 2002, originally a project of Ryze. com (a San Francisco-based tech business site), it was meant to rival Match.com, which had done extremely well as an online dating site. Friendster introduced the ability to view friends of friends. This was in large part due to their philosophy that people who shared friends would make better romantic partners than complete strangers. Friendster's buzz somewhat fizzled after other websites, which were not primarily focused on social networking but on media, like Flickr, Last.FM and YouTube, added these kinds of function to their sites. Yet it remains the most popular social network site in Southeast Asia.

In 2003 MySpace launched. While it garnered almost no traditional media attention, it was able to acquire a core, critical mass of members, especially estranged Friendster users who were upset not only at Friendster's spotty servers, leaving them unable to access the website when they wanted, but also what seemed like draconian use policies (such as the inability to create profiles for non-individuals such as bands and organizations). Many mainstream histories of MySpace focus on the early adoption by bands and their fans. But as boyd and Ellison note in their history of social network sites, this is not something that MySpace did with any clear intent. For the most part, bands made up a significant ratio of the contingent disaffected with Friendster, as it did not allow profiles for non-individuals. Hence, MySpace was the space to which many flocked.

Quickly realizing why so many ex-Friendster users were making the switch, MySpace succeeded by adopting many features that were recommended by users and, crucially, allowing users to personalize the look and function of their profiles by not restricting users from adding HTML. This contributes to MySpace's rather "messy" reputation today. In 2004, as the average price of a personal computer was dipping below the $1,000 mark, teens, many of whom had access to computers at school or at home, were moving onto MySpace in droves.

Facebook, which today is the world's largest social network site, started as a social network for students of Harvard University only. It later expanded to a group of colleges, then to all colleges, and, finally, to everyone, including non-individuals such as organizations, bands, etc. Its success came largely from the balance of aesthetic uniformity (Facebook profiles look nearly identical, with some variation due to third-party applications). Facebook maintains great success having incorporated many features of the social network sites that came before it. Rather brilliantly, it added a means by which to upload, store digital photos, and also "tag" people. (Tagging is described in detail in the previous chapter.)

Social network sites do not rely on creating a "second life," that is, creating another identity, or multiple identities. On the contrary, "what makes social network sites unique is not that they allow individuals to meet strangers, but rather that they enable users to articulate and make visible their social networks." What is implied is that social network sites facilitate the visualization of users' pre-existing, *offline* social networks. If there is an element of meeting strangers, it can be found in the list of connections sometimes called "Friends," or some variation, that allows one to look at friends of friends and then, if he or she so chooses, to befriend (that is, make a formal connection on the social network site) them.

The fulcrum, or "backbone" as boyd and Ellison call it, of social network sites is the profile. The profile is where individuals present themselves to others and where much of the interactions between friends and friends of friends occur. It is where most of what boyd refers to as "impression management" occurs. When an individual joins a social network site such as Facebook, she has to fill out a variety of forms and questions that deal with not only biographical information but also taste. Thus, on Facebook, the questions have to do with age, location, education, workplace, and gender but also favorite movies and televisions shows. On the profile is, crucially, a graph, a "public display of connections" showing with whom that particular person is also a friend. This is the second step when joining a social network site. One must "Friend," "Contact," "Fan," or "Follow" (depending on what a particular site may call this action) people whom you know.

On Facebook, there is the additional feature of "Friends in common," which shows the shared connections between the user and the profile owner.

As boyd and Ellison among many other social media researchers rightly note, the profile is where one "writes" herself into being. Although boyd and Ellison stress the fluidity of offline and online relationships in social network sites, there is considerable flexibility in how one chooses to write him- or herself into social network existence. It is indeed an exercise in self-curating, as Facebook, for instance, also allows for a "Wall," where friends may leave comments, links, and other media. In Facebook, one's tagged photos also appear on the wall. The user, however, does have the ability to remove any or all objects from his or her wall. He or she then becomes a curator of his or her Facebook self, who is able to remove embarrassingly silly, albeit admittedly cute, YouTube link of a French bulldog puppy unable to pick itself up from lying down, when he or she knows that a potential employer will be checking his or her Facebook profile. Although this is but one example of a profile in a single social network site, with Facebook's recent policy of attributing stable URLs for every user profile, we see that Facebook sees itself as not simply users presenting themselves to other members of their social network but to the World Wide Web more broadly.

More widely, boyd and Ellison view the rise of social network sites as indicative of a "shift in the organization of online communities"—from communities of interest to communities of people:

> Early public online communities such as . . . public discussion forums were structured by topics or according to topical hierarchies, but social network sites are structured as personal (or "egocentric") networks, with the individual at the center of their [sic] own community.
>
> *(boyd & Ellison 2007, p.9)*

Although "egocentrism" sounds quite catchy, in our view, it misses the point of what is really going on in social network sites.

Implicit in boyd and Ellison's pronouncement of social network sites functioning in a egocentric manner is that social network sites are increasingly focused on the profile, and, therefore, on the *self*. This may have been true. However, in the few years since the article's publication, much has occurred to affect the trajectory of social network sites and, more broadly, the organization of sociality.

Perhaps, the most important development has been the "decomputeri-zation" of social network sites and Internet use in general. This is covered in greater detail in the following chapter, but we should briefly explain what we mean by this: many social network sites are no longer assuming that users are behind a computer. Instead, they are not only assuming but are actively encouraging users to be able to connect to their social networks in a variety of technological means. Facebook, for instance, has applications (or "apps") that work on a variety of mobile platforms including BlackBerry, iPhone, iPad, and Droid, just to mention the most popular. Therefore, it is not unusual to see someone on Facebook on his or her mobile device.

This forces us to rethink a couple of things about boyd and Ellison's discussion of social network sites. For one, we must ask whether can we continue to call Facebook and Twitter, for example, social network *sites*. Indeed, they both have URLs and an extensive Web-based interface in which to participate. However, Twitter, for example, which relies on its users being to able update what they are doing at the moment, would not have had the kind of success that it does, with "190 million users tweeting 65 million times a day" (Schonfeld 2010). For example, Posterous is a free Web service that allows users to post content onto various Web platforms—blogs, Facebook, Twitter, etc. via email. Thus, one could theoretically be posting to various Web outlets without even having access to the Web. One of Posterous' most impressive features is that it automatically formats any file format or Web link and converts it to a readable, Web-friendly format. So if a Posterous user wishes to post a YouTube video on all his or her social networks including Facebook, Twitter and Tumblr, all he or she needs to do is send the URL of the video to an email account associated with Posterous. This could all happen via mobile phone.

Furthermore, what has emerged is the widespread ability to share links on social network sites without having to be at the URL of the particular site. In 2009 Facebook introduced "Facebook Connect," which allows for Facebook accounts to be linked and accessible anywhere on the open Web (Arrington 2008b). So if one is a regular at the American liberal political blog *The Huffington Post*, he or she does not need to be at Facebook's URL (http://www.facebook.com/) in order to post a particular article or post on her profile. Nearly all content-oriented websites and blogs now have sharing widgets with links to Facebook, Twitter, and email so that the user can share the post quickly. The idea is to have access to one's social network throughout the Web, not only in the particular space of the social network site's URL.

The technological development that is directly responsible for the delinking of social networks from the Web is API or application programming interface. *PC Magazine*'s encyclopedia defines API as:

> A language and message format used by an application program to communicate with the operating system or some other control program such as a database management system (DBMS) or communications protocol. APIs are implemented by writing function calls in the program, which provide the linkage to the required subroutine for execution. Thus, an API implies that some program module is available in the computer to perform the operation or that it must be linked into the existing program to perform the tasks.
>
> *(PC Magazine n.d.)*

API has been around since, well, computer programming itself. Why API is so significant for understanding Web 2.0 is that it is pretty much customary or web services to open it up. This allows for not only third-party developers to write programs for various social networks but it also facilitates communication between social network sites. Thus, there is now a slew of applications that support Facebook, applications that are not developed or overseen by Facebook itself.

Twitter is the social network that has had by far the most enthusiastic reception by programmers—both professional and hobbyists, many of whom have found amazingly creative ways to integrate Twitter's API. An especially genius, although largely impractical, application was achieved by Justin Wickett, who posted a video of him being able to turn off his bedroom lights via Twitter on his account on Vimeo, a video-sharing site in the vein of YouTube but catered towards film makers. Using Twitter's API, a computer, and a couple of other programs that allowed his computer and the lights to communicate, Wickett was able to tweet "Turn off bedroom lights," and have the lights in his bedroom go off. While this may be more than a bit unnecessary, it nevertheless shows how important opening up APIs have been for the current regime of social networking.

In addition to what we are calling the "de-Webification of social networks," we believe Twitter to exemplify another regime of sociality whereby the primary locus of interaction no longer remains the profile but the feed. If one has a Twitter account, the home page resembles an RSS feed or even a blog, with backwards, chronological listing of updates or "Tweets" from people whom the user "follows." Follow means that the user "subscribes" (to use another term from RSS) to another user's tweets; so everything that the person being followed tweets will appear on the home page of the follower. Unlike Facebook, Twitter's friending system therefore is unidirectional not bidirectional. (Although, by default, all Twitter accounts are public, one can choose to make his or her Twitter account private, which would mean that one would have to approve requests to follow them individually.) Just as an RSS reader would accumulate the various blogs and websites that the user subscribes to and place it in a unified interface with the most recent posts/articles/entries at the top, the home page of a Twitter user lists the tweets from the various users whom the person follows with the most recent at the top.

Although the dynamic of self-presentation on social networks undoubtedly still remains, as it cannot go anywhere since at root social life is always social performance, it has changed significantly in recent years. The profile is no longer at the heart of the interaction neither on Twitter nor, due to its recent changes to mimic the user experience of Twitter, on Facebook. Facebook's new "home page" (or the page that is opened when one logs into Facebook is, in their parlance, the "News Feed," described as "[highlighting] what's happening in your social circles on Facebook. It updates a personalized list of news stories throughout the day, so you'll know when Mark adds Britney Spears to his Favorites or when your crush is single again. Now, whenever you log in, you'll get the latest headlines generated by the activity of your friends and social groups" (Sanghvi 2006).

The net effect of this shift in how social network sites work is a new form of sociality that, we suggest, is particular to the current moment in the history of the World Wide Web and in social media more broadly. If the moment that boyd and Ellison so aptly pointed out and analyzed was the "identity-driven" moment of social network sites, we are entering (or already in) a different moment, one of "social ambiance."

Social ambiance of social networks

It is the feed, *not* the profile, that we believe to be signaling a shift in the recent trends of social networks away from what boyd and Ellison call "egocentric" towards what French sociologist Michel Maffesoli calls "social ambiance" (Maffesoli 1993). This shift consists of two interrelated aspects: (1) liveness, or contemporaneity and (2) social proprioception. Twitter, along with some other social network services, are, we believe, at the forefront of this new sociality.

In a 2007 article in *Wired*, technology writer Clive Thompson gives what we view as the most apt analysis of the sociality of Twitter. Twitter, he says, is like "social proprioception" (Thompson 2007). It gives the feeling of a "social sixth sense." This feeling of sociality as feeling has mostly to do with how users are encouraged by Twitter to use it. The heading above the text box on one's Twitter home page is "What's happening?" This can be, and indeed has been, interpreted quite loosely by many users. Tweets range from the utterly banal to "On the toilet. It's a big one," to "Check out this article. [URL]." As Thompson writes:

> The messages [on Twitter] are limited to 140 characters, so they lean toward pithy, haiku-like utterances. When I dropped by the main Twitter page, people had posted notes like "Doing lunch and picking up father-in-law from senior center." Or "Checking out *Ghost Whisperer*" or simply "Thinking I'm old."
>
> *(Thompson 2007)*

As he goes on to note, it is like blogging but "taken to the supremely banal extreme." As a member of my dissertation committee, whose introduction to the world of social networks I facilitated, commented to me, "Why is someone saying, 'I'm in the tub, having a bubble bath.'? But then again, why am *I* reading it?" (After Twitter's rather well-noted rise in user base, Facebook responded by attempting to create a very similar effect in March 2009 (Schonfeld 2009).) But it is in the banality and the mundane where Thompson locates the sway of Twitter and why so many people are self-described addicts:

> Individually, most Twitter messages are stupefyingly trivial. But the true value of Twitter ... is cumulative. The power is in the surprising effects that come from receiving thousands of pings from your posse. And this, it turns out, suggests where the Web is heading.

It this cumulative effect that Thompson likens to proprioception, the ability of the human body to know where its limbs are. This, as he notes, is necessary for bodily orientation, and is what keeps one from being a *klutz*, to use a Yiddish saying. "Twitter and other constant-contact media," he writes, "create *social* proprioception." It creates a sense of "tactility" in social relations. It is not the embodiment of "hipster narcissism," as some critics suggest—their line of reasoning being something like "Why would anyone care what you are doing or thinking at any given moment?"—but as Thompson suggests "the real appeal of Twitter is almost the inverse of narcissism. It's practically collectivist—you're creating a shared under-standing larger than yourself" (Thompson 2007).

Additionally, this trend towards social proprioception can be most readily seen in particular events in which Twitter became particularly influ-ential in acting as a means of news sharing and even collective grief. An event that garnered a lot of attention in the United States at least was the emergency landing of a US Airways plane in New York City's Hudson River in January 2009 (Wald 2009). Most of the news stories involved praising the pilot for landing the plane safely on the Hudson River and the crew for managing to get all passengers off the plane safely. However, there was substory regarding where the first photos of the event came from—Twitter. Janis Krums, a Twitter user from Florida, happened to be on the Staten Island Ferry, as it was diverted from its usual route from Battery Park in Lower Manhattan to St. George Station on Staten Island to retrieve passengers of the plane. Using TwitPic, a service that allows one to post photos via Twitter, Krums uploaded perhaps the first photograph of the landing site with the following message: "http://twitpic.com/135xa – There's a plane in the Hudson. I'm on the ferry going to pick up the people. Crazy" (Krums 2009). This picture was then widely circulated through the mainstream news media channels that we usually expect to have had the scoop. With resources such as helicopters and long-lens cameras, it was odd that a completely private citizen, that is, one not employed by the news media, was able to do such a thing.

Another example to this effect that Thompson gives is the death of Michael Jackson on June 25, 2009 (Thompson 2009). This event was far less about "citizen journalism" or "crowdsourcing" (Howe 2008) as the previous example was but rather the way in which particular news events are shared and reflected on through Twitter. Soon after Jackson's death was reported, by American celebrity news and gossip website TMZ.com no less, many took to Twitter to start sharing their favorite Jackson songs, using, for example, YouTube, which is a repository of many cultural artifacts, Michael Jackson and Jackson 5 video footage included, and grieve. As one of the few studies on Jackson's death and Twitter reports, "at its peak, the conversation about Michael Jackson's death on Twitter proceeded at a rate of 78 tweets per second" (Kim & Gilbert 2009).

According to Thompson, the qualitative difference of sociality on the Web today marks a shift towards what many media critics have called "real-time Web." Thompson again:

> For more than 10 years, Google has organized the Web by figuring out who has authority. The company measures which sites have the most links pointing to them—crucial votes of confidence—and checks to see whether a site grew to prominence slowly and organically, which tends to be a marker of quality. If a site amasses a zillion links overnight, it's almost certainly spam.
>
> But the real-time Web behaves in the opposite fashion. It's all about "trending topics"—zOMG a plane crash!—which by their very nature generate a massive number of links and postings within minutes. And a search engine can't spend days deciding what is the most crucial site or posting; people want to know immediately.
>
> *(Thompson 2009)*

Thompson here touches on a couple of important points. First, the real-time Web, as exemplified by the place of Twitter in the US Airways plane crash, has shifted the authority orientation of a Google-dominated Web. The importance and success of Google's search can be traced to, as he rightly notes, a distribution of "reliability." When we google something, we assume that the top results are what we want. But when events such as a plane landing on the Hudson River, or when the biggest global pop star in the last few decades reportedly suddenly dies, there is a massive push by users of the Web to seek information, any information, on the event. Information, in this context, is not simply something worth reading or official reporting but anything that pertains to the event. For Thompson, this marks a different kind of Web than the one dominated by search. Even in 2005 Microsoft had major plans to try to create a search alternative to Google (BBC News 2005). Search was *synonymous* with the World Wide Web. Yet today, the search wars have largely ended with Google and other Internet companies moving on to apps and cloud computing. To paraphrase Edo Segal, search organized our memory; real-time Web organizes our consciousness (as quoted in Thompson 2009).

So what does real-time Web mean for the slower, search-based Web of which blogs and other page-based communities are constitutive part? Is the model of online sociality no longer blog communities and forums?

Online communities?

October 26, 2009 is an important date in the history of sociality on the World Wide Web. It marked the end of GeoCities, "an online community of user-created Web pages from the early days of the Internet," as one article described it (Connelly 2009). For those of us who could remember, GeoCities was one of the first places where you could create a personal Web page, with an actual URL (although these tended to be quite long and bulky). Started in 1994 as Beverly Hills Internet (BHI), GeoCities remediated the experience of neighborhoods in "real" cities in the form of thematic categories, "including 'Sunset Strip' for rock and punk music, 'Wall Street' for personal finance and investing, and 'Area 51' for science fiction" (Connelly 2009).

Seen as a precursor to today's blogs and social networks, the end of GeoCities was a cause for reflection for many who study and write about the Web but had long forgotten about how the earliest social formations on the Web looked. In fact, most did not know that GeoCities was still around. After its purchase by Yahoo!, GeoCities did not make much news. But when Yahoo! announced early in 2009 that it would close GeoCities to most users (it's still available in Japan), many began to reflect on the death of page-based online communities, of which GeoCities was clearly an innovator. As Pheobe Connelly of *The American Prospect* writes:

> The geographic nomenclature of GeoCities gave those new to the Internet a familiar shorthand for how social interaction could unfold. Sure, the tools might be different, but the concept of neighbors and like-minded groups of people, would, GeoCities promised, operate the same online as in the real world. Our desire

for community is an insight key to many successful online ventures that have come after. Facebook lets users "become a fan" of bands, magazines, and businesses, join groups that petition for health-care reform, and organize high school reunions. Blogs organize themselves into like-minded groups known as rings, even holding "carnivals" where all bloggers involved publish entries on a set them.

The demise of GeoCities is not just the disappearance of a gif-riddled online ghost town—it's the death of a pioneering online community.

(Connelly 2009)

While there is very little doubt that GeoCities was influential as the framework on which many Web 2.0 social formations modeled themselves—wittingly or not, it seems that Connelly uses the term "community" specifically when describing GeoCities. For her, one joined GeoCities not merely to create a personal Web page but to join a "community of users."

But what *is* a community and how does one recognize it online?

This question, of measuring connectivity, is one that has been around since the beginning of sociology as a discipline. Émile Durkheim, considered by some to be the "founder of sociology" (in that he was the first to found a department of sociology in Europe), asked a rather Hobbesian question: how would post-traditional societies maintain in the tumult of capitalism when the regulating action of religion's moral guidelines have waned? It is from these questions that the concepts of "solidarity" and "social bond" emerged.

Arguably, Durkheim's question is one that has been debated by intellectuals throughout the history of modernity, through the analytic of "community." Many social scientists look to early German sociologist Ferdinand Tonnies' typology of social groups—*Gemeinschaft* and *Gesellschaft*, which roughly translates to "community" and "society," or at least that is how it has been received, probably all too reductively, in the United States. This typology has had a specific influence on sociological and popular discussions of the shift in social relations and modernity, and, implicitly, technology. The example given by Tonnies for the ideal type "community" was the rural village, while, for "society," it was a business. What was gleaned from this was that there was an eventual replacement of "community" with "society" as the dominant form of association in the shift from "traditional" societies to "modern" societies.

Durkheim framed this question in terms of solidarity. For him, and confusingly for many students of sociology, *mechanical* solidarity described the bond of traditional societies, which relied on kinship and familial ties. In calling this "mechanical," Durkheim, it seems, wished to convey the "automatic" nature of the social positions that largely determined social relations. *Organic* solidarity described modern or industrial societies. "Organic" refers to the cooperation of component parts for the good of the greater social order, much like the different organs work together for the maintenance of the human body.

Community, therefore, remains as the default way of thinking about social relations. Well into the era of Web 2.0, websites, blogs, and social networks are described as "communities." In fact, we have come to a point where "social network" is used interchangeably with "online community." A video interview on BBC News' technology section with Biz Stone and Evan Williams, the founders of Twitter, includes this line in the description: "Katty Kay spoke with its co-founders Biz Stone and Evan Williams about the ever growing *community* that is living online" (Stone & Williams 2010; emphasis added). Although this may seem like a minor issue, we are suggesting that it is a blasé elision that seems to occur with such great frequency that represents a widespread acceptance of "community" as the ideal form of social relations today.

Why the fascination with community? Is it simply because pre-Internet social relations were understood in such a way? But that cannot be since even the works of the sociologists just mentioned suggest that "community" is long gone.

As mentioned earlier, since its inception, the World Wide Web has been founded on a principle of potential connectivity conceived of chiefly as communication. This could also be said of other, much older, media such as speech. As many scholars of media and writing have noted, writing was in large part considered to be a downgrade in relation to speech. In other words, writing, from the earliest forms of script, which communications scholar, theologian and friend to Marshall McLuhan Walter Ong argues may be traced back to the Sumerians, to pictographic, ideographic and alphabetic writing systems, was seen mainly as a way to simply record the content of speech, which in the west has been traditionally seen as having a certain "affinity with thought," as he puts it (Ong 1967, p.138). For Ong, communication is narrowly defined as the transmission of thought, that is, the "meeting" of one interior mind with another. Thus, he writes:

> The historical fact is that the world of sound (which, as we have seen is of course associated to some degree with the tactile and especially the kinesthetic) has proved in all cultures the most immediate sensory coefficient of thought ... One can readily discern several reasons why this is so: connections between sound, thought, and communication; connections between sound, thought, truth, and time; connections between the structure of predication itself and vocalization.
>
> *(Ong 1967, p.140)*

He goes on to detail each set of connections in greater detail but of interest here is how the alignment of sound and interiority affect sociality:

> As has been earlier suggested, a spoken language unites communities as nothing else does. The psychological reasons for this are by no means all understood. But one reason is certainly the interiorizing quality of sound and thus of voice. Voice, as has been explained, manifests interiors as interiors and unites them ... [S]ince a human community is essentially a union of interior consciousnesses.
>
> *(Ong 1967, p.146)*

And indeed, if we are to take Ong at his word (since he is not alone in thinking this way as the dominant history of the west in many ways reflects his privileging of sound over sight), the history of media becomes a history of alienation, of interference, or individualization, with the cost to "community" remaining barely implicit.

But, as Ong himself noted, "communication" is really no longer the goal (or "vocation" as the sociologist Max Weber may have suggested) of contemporary technological media, since at least radio, which he, along with McLuhan argued, had a "retribalizing" effect (McLuhan 1969). Indeed, to be able to communicate is the basic assumption in Internet use. Thus what characterizes the connectivity particular to Web 2.0 is not primarily communicative, in the sense of one-to-one interaction but, as we suggest, ambient or what the early social theorist Max Scheler called "fellow feeling" (Scheler 1983).

This is evident in not only social network sites per se but also in sites such as Daily Kos, a well-known progressive (or "liberal" as we Americans say) political blog and website that is often associated with what in mainstream political discourse is dubbed the "netroots." The term "netroots" refers to a relatively loose assemblage of blogs and websites that have liberal-left political tendencies. Daily Kos, started in 2002 by Markos Moulitsas, boasts 2.5 million unique visitors a month and a quarter of a million registered users, according to its "About" page. It is also the inspiration for the yearly "Netroots Nation" Convention, which used to be known as the YearlyKos Convention. Although Daily Kos is not what one thinks of as a typical social networking site, there is no doubt that it is, indeed, a social network.

At the heart of the Daily Kos, as Carlo Scannella argues, is the eventual mundane nature of the experience of the interacting there. He does not use the word "mundane" disparagingly but does so to describe the quotidian nature of social formations on the Web. The participation that is facilitated by Web 2.0 and the talk about *social* media is not necessarily about greater emotional investment in these media. "For its users," Scannella argues, "the Daily Kos website requires continual interaction and engagement, as the list of current diaries [posts] is constantly being refreshed and revised—the site is built on a never-ending stream of commentary, and users check in throughout the day, to 'catch up' on the latest news, and to see if others have responded to their comments and diaries." An experience of this sort creates a "regular practice, a rhythm . . . within which participants feel rooted, a virtual space through which they are formed into a network of relations that constitute the basis of a strong sense of community shared at Daily Kos" (Scanella 2008). Therefore, the figure of the Japanese *otaku*, the obsessive kid who is on the computer or video game system all day (what is so different about an adult at work who is on the computer all day?), is merely a caricature of how media technologies become incorporated into humans' very state of being.

It is because social formations on Web 2.0 create a sense of "fellow feeling" through low-intensity investment that we believe the term "community" must be reevaluated. While many social networks describe themselves as "communities" (even Daily Kos calls itself "the premier online political community"), it is a term that we find to be of little use. For one, "community" too often connotes an outmoded understanding of social cohesion, one rooted in shared culture, language, ethnicity, and, most importantly, geography. This reality has not ever really existed. It is a false nostalgia that harks back to a time when social differences did not exist. But even in the most "traditional" of societies, scholars have shown a high level of social differentiation and hierarchy. Therefore, to refer to some past where "everybody knows your name" is, in our view, somewhat disingenuous. Additionally, "community" is too often reified as the unattainable, yet highly desirable, *telos* of social relations in political and academic discourse. In the USA, one hears complaints of "lack of community," especially in academic works dealing with growing political disaffection. The key work in this regard is Robert Putnam's *Bowling Alone*, which bemoans the hyper-individualized state of social reality.

In a rather bizarre twist of fate, as we have argued in this chapter, it seems the opposite has come to be in light of Web 2.0. The individual or user is perhaps hyper-socialized. And without a doubt, there have been significant critiques expressing concern for the encroachment of the solitude of the individual psyche due to the ever-growing complexity of social networks. (This is discussed in greater detail along with other lines of criticisms of Web 2.0 in Chapter 5.) Access to a computer is no longer necessary, as social networks have developed applications or "apps" for a variety of mobile devices. Social networking is no longer something that one does sitting in front of a computer but rather when walking down the street, providing a very different phenomenological experience for the user.

It is to this that we will turn in the following chapter.

References

Arrington, M., 2008a. Facebook No Longer The Second Largest Social Network, *TechCrunch*. Available at: http://techcrunch.com/2008/06/12/facebook-no-longer-the-second-largest-social-network/. [Accessed July 21, 2010.]

——, 2008b. Facebook Responds To MySpace With Facebook Connect, *TechCrunch*. Available at: http://techcrunch.com/2008/05/09/facebook-responds-to-myspace-with-facebook-connect/. [Accessed July 22, 2010.]

BBC News, 2005. Microsoft Aims to Trounce Google, *BBC*. Available at: http://news.bbc.co.uk/2/hi/technology/4382112.stm. [Accessed July 25, 2010.]

boyd, d. & Ellison, N., 2007. Social Network Sites: Definition, History, and Scholarship, *Journal of Computer-Mediated Communication*, 13(1). Available at:

http://jcmc.indiana.edu/vol13/issue1/boyd.ellison.html. [Accessed July 17, 2010.]

Cellan-Jones, R., 2009. Twitter and a Classic Picture, *dot.life*. Available at: http://www.bbc.co.uk/blogs/technology/2009/01/twitter_and_a_classic_picture.html. [Accessed July 24, 2010.]

Connelly, P., 2009. The Life and Death of Online Communities | The American Prospect, *The American Prospect*. Available at: http://www.prospect.org/cs/articles?article=neo_cities. [Accessed July 26, 2010.]

Daily Kos, Daily Kos, About Daily Kos. Available at: http://www.dailykos.com/special/about2#dk. [Accessed July 15, 2010.]

Granovetter, M.S., 1973. The Strength of Weak Ties, *American Journal of Sociology*, 78(6), 1360–80.

Howe, J., 2008. *Crowdsourcing: Why the Power of the Crowd Is Driving the Future of Business* 1st edn, Crown Business.

Kim, E. & Gilbert, S., 2009. *Detecting Sadness in 140 Characters*. Available at: http://www.webecologyproject.org/2009/08/detecting-sadness-in-140-characters/. [Accessed July 24, 2010.]

Kittler, F., 1996. The History of Communication Media, *CTheory*, (ga114). Available at: http://www.ctheory.net/articles.aspx?id=45. [Accessed July 16, 2010.]

Krums, J., 2009. Twitter / Janis Krums: http://twitpic.com/135xa – ... *Twitter*. Available at: http://twitter.com/jkrums/status/1121915133. [Accessed July 24, 2010.]

Maffesoli, M., 1993. The Social Ambiance, *Current Sociology*, 41(2), 1–15.

McLuhan, M., 1969. Marshall McLuhan—A Candid Conversation with the High Priest of Popcult and Metaphysician of Media, *Playboy*, March, 233–69.

Moore, T., 2003. Camp Aims to Beat Web Addiction, *BBC*. Available at: http://news.bbc.co.uk/2/hi/europe/3125475.stm. [Accessed July 15, 2010.]

Ong, W.J., 2002. *Orality and Literacy: The Technologizing of the Word*, Routledge.

——, 1967. *The Presence of the Word: Some Prolegomena for Cultural and Religious History*, Yale University Press.

PC Magazine, API, *PCMag.com Encyclopedia*. Available at: http://www.pcmag.com/encyclopedia_term/0,2542,t=API&i=37856,00.asp. Accessed July 22, 2010.]

Rheingold, H., 2000. *The Virtual Community: Homesteading on the Electronic Frontier* rev. edn, MIT Press.

Sanders, J., Nee, V., & Sernau, S., 2002. Asian Immigrants' Reliance on Social Ties in a Multiethnic Labor Market, *Social Forces*, 81, 281.

Sanghvi, R., 2006. Facebook Gets a Facelift | Facebook, *The Facebook Blog*. Available at: http://blog.facebook.com/blog.php?post=2207967130. [Accessed July 23, 2010.]

Scanella, C., 2008. *Mundane Blogging: The Medium and Social Practices of Daily Kos*, New York: New School.

Scheler, M.F., 1983. *Nature of Sympathy* 3rd edn, Shoe String Press, Inc.

Schonfeld, E., 2010. Costolo: Twitter Now Has 190 Million Users Tweeting 65 Million Times A Day, *TechCrunch*. Available at: http://techcrunch.com/2010/06/08/twitter-190-million-users/. [Accessed July 21, 2010.]

——, 2009. Facebook's Response To Twitter, *TechCrunch*. Available at: http://techcrunch.com/2009/03/04/facebooks-response-to-twitter/. [Accessed July 23, 2010.]

Sillito, D., 2009. Twitter's Iconic Image of US Airways Plane, *BBC News*. Available at: http://news.bbc.co.uk/2/hi/americas/7834755.stm. [Accessed July 24, 2010.]

Stone, B., 2008. Control Lights with Twitter, *Twitter Blog*. Available at: http://blog.twitter.com/2008/05/control-lights-with-twitter.html. [Accessed July 22, 2010.]

Stone, B. & Williams, E., 2010. Is Twitter a Force for Good? Available at: http://www.bbc.co.uk/news/technology-10652690. [Accessed July 19, 2010.]

Thompson, C., 2009. Clive Thompson on How the Real-Time Web Is Leaving Google Behind, *Wired*, 17(10). Available at: http://www.wired.com/techbiz/people/magazine/17-10/st_thompson. [Accessed July 24, 2010.]

——, 2007. Clive Thompson on How Twitter Creates a Social Sixth Sense, *Wired*, 15(07). Available at: http://www.wired.com/techbiz/media/magazine/15-07/st_thompson. [Accessed July 13, 2010.]

Turkle, S., 1997. *Life on the Screen: Identity in the Age of the Internet*, Simon & Schuster.

Wald, M.L., 2009. Plane Crew is Credited for Nimble Reaction, *New York Times*. Available at: http://www.nytimes.com/2009/01/16/nyregion/16pilot.html. [Accessed July 24, 2010.]

Wickett, J. 2010. Control Lights with Twitter, *Vimeo*. Available at: http://vimeo.com/1025711. [Accessed July 22, 2010.]

4

THE EXPERIENCE OF WEB 2.0

A techno-phenomenology of multi-tasking and mobility

Let us start with two stories reported in the news in the latter half of 2010. The first is from New York City:

> The residents of 165 Pinehurst Avenue in the Washington Heights section of Manhattan were in a bit of a dilemma. Their building was crumbling beneath their feet. They needed to fix the problem. Their 82-year-old building was increasingly hazardous. So why did they not act immediately? Well, it would have meant that the remarkable cellphone reception that they all had in the building would be jeopardized. See, they believed that the problem arose from the recent installation of two cellphone base stations and twenty antennas on the roof. As the New York Times article which reported this story notes, the residents had "something most modern Americans would envy: impeccable cellphone service".
>
> *(Buckley & Richtel 2010)*

As those of us who have spent some time in New York know, the city is renowned for having many dead zones (areas where there is almost no cellphone service), particularly in older buildings. It is one of the most immediate differences between it and other global cities such as London or Seoul. New York's subways lack cellphone service. Good reception is at a premium here and the mobile carriers all know it. In 2004 Verizon, a major American telecommunications company, launched a popular ad campaign featuring a fictional Verizon Wireless employee who goes around to different places—the bus, the grocery store, the elevator— repeating what is, at least in the USA, an incantation of the mobile generation, "Can you hear me now?"

Here is another story, this one from the UK:

> The average Briton spends almost half their waking life using media and communications. Ofcom, the independent communications regulator in the UK, similar to the US Federal Communications Commission (FCC), released a report finding that people in the UK spend seven hours and five minutes of the average day's time awake of fifteen hours and forty five minutes using their phones, watching TV and on the computer. But, as the report notes, most people spend far more time on media and communications cramming the equivalent of nine hours by multi-tasking on several devices at once.
>
> *(Cellan–Jones 2010a)*

In many ways, these two stories summarize the experience of Web 2.0. The former shows the importance of the technological infrastructure that is the "silent partner" of the proliferation of mobile computing. But more, it demonstrates a new "way of being," one that relies on technological and communicative access as much as it does on shelter (perhaps making a push for the reconsideration of such "basic needs" as food, water, clothing, shelter and mobile phone reception). Le Corbusier famously once said, "A house is machine for living in." In the case of 165 Pinehurst Avenue, the house and the machine are entangled in what seems to be a zero-sum game.

While the Ofcom report's headline, so to speak, is the sheer number of hours that Britons spend using media technologies, it is also a story about the changing abilities and capacities of technological human beings in the age of Web 2.0. As the report notes, among the young, multi-tasking is undoubtedly the norm and commonplace. There is no such thing as *just* talking on the phone or *just* watching television. There is usually some other activity occurring while doing so. As mentioned in the previous chapter, certain televised events, whether it is a sporting event—the 2010

World Cup, for instance, actually negatively affected Twitter service—or the news coverage of the death of a pop star, result in traffic spikes on social networking sites. This could only occur with people multi-tasking. The entire complex of Web 2.0 is dependent on this fact.

Just as these two stories equally reflect the seriousness with which people on either side of the Atlantic treat their media technologies, they also serve as good starting points for the two main processes under discussion in this chapter—multi-tasking and mobility. In doing so, we attempt what social theorist Scott Lash calls a "technological phenomenology." This will involve an analysis of Web 2.0 *in use* with special attention paid to *experience*. For Lash, the importance of phenomenology, as an approach to study technology, can be found when looking back on phenomenology's original critique of the assumptions of the dominant strands of philosophical analysis at the time. "At the heart of the phenomenological revolution against the subject-object thinking, against the positivism of representational culture, is the notion of *intentionality*," he writes. Intentionality effectively did away with the idea of an objective observer, a disembodied subject that coolly looks on his object without pretense. "'Intentionality' means that the subject is already in the world with the object:"

> In two-world [non-endogenous] models of knowledge you observer of judge. In one-world models you experience. Phenomenology, in contradistinction to realism, holds that there are no objects except for an "experiencer." There are no objects, no meaning, no truth and no knowledge in the absence of such an experiencer in the world with objects … The experiencer … has knowledge of the object from his/her attitude, from the particular perspective of his intentionality. This knowledge is not through judgment, but takes place in a mode in which judgment is suspended: it is instead knowledge through belief.
>
> *(Lash 2002, p.165)*

What is important about this perspective, in Lash's view, is that experience comes to the forefront.

And in the course of this chapter, we will stick close to the experience of Web 2.0, as thus far we have only broached some of its technical and formal aspects. We attempt to show the *immersive* and *ubiquitous* quality of

Web 2.0, focusing particularly on multi-tasking, and its technical conditions of possibility, and mobility, as well as what has facilitated this mobile experience, namely location-based social networking software, as well as Wi-Fi. We conclude with a brief discussion of "spreadable media," a term that many tech analysts use to describe the way in which media content moves online, in lieu of the "viral" metaphor that perhaps maintains a hegemonic position. The "experience" of Web 2.0 is, we hope to argue, one that is far removed from the idea of computing as "living elsewhere," that is, separate from empirical reality. To put it in philosophical terms, the chapter aims to show the flattened ontology—the endogeneity—of computing today.

Multi-tasking

Multi-tasking is a term that today refers to human behavior, for better or for worse, appearing most frequently in cover letters to employers, as a means of self-description. But, as the *Oxford English Dictionary* shows, it was first used in reference to "the performance by a computer of a number of different tasks or jobs concurrently (as by interleaving or multi-processing)" in a 1968 issue of *Datamation* magazine. It was only around 2000 that the term reached widespread use (at least according to the editors of the *OED*) to describe human productivity (OED Online 2010).

While this may seem like another instance of technological metaphors gone too far and expressing a technological determinism, it is, on the contrary, evidence of a "convergence," although not one where we look to the work of Henry Jenkins first but to that of Donna Haraway. The fact that multi-tasking described the activity of computers and now with regard to human activity is undoubtedly a coming together of some kind, which Haraway would undoubtedly call a "hybrid." Indeed, since cyberneticist Norbert Wiener's *Cybernetics*, there have been innumerable attempts by scientists and philosophers to look for a common thread that weaves together machines and humans. Haraway's and Bruno Latour's respective oeuvres do this most formidably in recent times. Without going too deeply into questions of ontology, although that may be just about impossible, what is clear is that they all assume that the meeting of technology and the human, a relationship that goes back to the "origins of humanity," as Andre Leroi-Gourhan would no doubt argue, affects both the human and "machine," or device. Of interest here is not whether the multi-tasking of the computer "created" the multi-tasking *habitus* of humans but how multi-tasking as an ethic of contemporary technological culture has developed both in hardware and culturally.

In the realm of devices, it is digitization and computerization that has had the most impact. In many ways, the onset of multi-tasking-as-*ethic* comes largely in parallel development with the remediation of many consumer electronics goods into smaller and smaller computers. This claim has, we admit, some dependence on Moore's Law, which states that the number of transistors that can be placed on an integrated circuit—thus, making devices smaller and faster—doubles every two years. The micro-processor undoubtedly plays a major role in what we are talking about here.

But multi-tasking is first and foremost a feature of most of today's consumer devices because they are, in fact, small computers. Smartphones and media players such as iPods, for instance, bear evidence to this fact. One major aspect of computing, as one clearly knows, when looking at the advent of the personal computer in the 1980s and then its popularization over the course of the 1990s, is that it was always oriented around multi-tasking. The PC, while still bearing some resemblance to the word processor (also called the electronic typewriter) in how it looked, differed greatly from it because of its multi-functionality. It was not a single-use machine. This is made clear in a semiotic analysis of even the earliest advertisements for PCs.

In a 1984 special Christmas-time commercial for the Tandy 1000 (with color monitor) sold at Radio Shack, a husband proudly shows his wife the gift he has purchased for the family. It's the computer, with a red bow on top. He explains, "Honey, this is just like the PC I have at the office!" "Oh!" she rejoices. What follows is a series of attempts by the husband to use the computer to no avail. His first try is thwarted as his wife is on the computer doing the family budget. Next, his daughter is finishing her report, which she assures him, "is due tomorrow." Finally, it is the husband's turn. With joystick in hand, he gleefully plays a computer game, as we hear the voice of his wife in another room (perhaps from the bedroom), "Don't stay up too late doing work, honey!" Like a child getting away with stealing, he yells back, "Don't worry. I won't!"

The intended meaning of this TV commercial is pretty clear. The computer can do so many things; there is something for *every*one in the family. Go buy one now!

This multi-functionality intensified, as personal computers not only grew faster and more powerful, thus allowing for more functions, but also smaller. This was the case as the 1990s saw laptop computers and, more importantly, PDAs (personal digital assistants)—the precursors to a whole generation of mobile, Internet-accessing peripherals such as iPods, smartphones and ebook readers—began to infiltrate the consumer market.

Computing, from its inception, and later computerization, produced a different kind of perceptual user experience from prior media technologies. A computer, while it mirrors the somewhat non-linear experience of radio and television, makes a somewhat harder break with those two prior media due to the great "input" that it demands of the user. While radio, cinema and television maintained an experiential singularity—the listener or viewer could listen to or watch only one station or channel at a time, the computer, as media theorist Alex Galloway notes, operates on a different principle—that of "windowing" (Friedberg 2006) or "morphing" (Manovich 2007). Galloway writes:

> This is one of the great aesthetic leaps of the graphical user interface beyond the example set by cinema: no longer will the viewer experience montage via cuts over time, proceeding from shot to shot; one must now "cut" within any given frame, holding two or more source images side by side, which themselves will persist montage-less over much longer "takes" than their cinematic predecessors. Fusing cuts within the frame replaces fusing cuts in time.
>
> *(Galloway 2007, p.21)*

Although Galloway here is speaking more to the changes in the general style of informatic representation, his comments summarize for us the disassembling or "deterritorialization," to use a term used frequently in cultural theory as per Gilles Deleuze and Felix Guattari (Deleuze & Guattari 1987), of perceptual experience with the onset of the digitization and computerization of devices. A recent article in the *New York Times* summarizes this point nicely:

> Today, traditional media companies face the adaptive challenge posed by the Internet. That challenge is not just the technology itself, but how it has altered people's habits of media consumption.

Multi-tasking, in the sense of truly being able to focus on more than one cognitively taxing task at a time, may well be a myth, experts say. But it does seem to be an accurate description of people's behavior— watching television, while surfing the Internet or answering text messages. "Consumers are getting much more adept at engaging two or three forms of media at a time," says Steve Hasker, head of Nielsen's media unit.

(Lohr 2010)

With computers no longer relegated to a box on top of a desk, but in our pockets, we see that multi-tasking, as technological feature and as *habitus*, has become dominant.

What else could explain the recent turn towards "apps" that has taken hold of so much mainstream media commentary? "Apps" (short for applications) refers to downloadable programs on a variety of smartphone platforms—the main ones currently being Apple's iOS, Google's Android, and RIM's BlackBerry OS. They have taken a central place in recent discussions sparked by *Wired* magazine editor-in-chief Chris Anderson's article "Web is Dead" (Anderson & Wolff 2010). There, Anderson and co-author Wolff suggest that "one of the most important shifts in the digital world has been the move from the wide-open Web to semiclosed platforms that use the Internet for transport but not the browser for display." They describe the contemporary technological experience in the following, very telling, way:

You wake up and check your email on your bedside iPad—that's one app. During breakfast you browse Facebook, Twitter, and the *New York Times*—three more apps. On the way to the office, you listen to a podcast on your smartphone. Another app. At work, you scroll through RSS feeds in a reader and have Skype and IM conversations. More apps. At the end of the day, you come home, make dinner while listening to Pandora, play some games on Xbox Live, and watch a movie on Netflix's streaming service.

(Anderson & Wolff 2010)

Suffice it to say that as much as they do to the claim that the Web is dead (a point to which we will return to in the following chapter), Anderson and

Wolff's words serve just as well as a phenomenology of the multi-tasking of today's mobile devices and humans.

Mobility

In recent years, scholars such as Mimi Sheller and John Urry, who have called for a "mobility turn" or "new mobilities paradigm" for future research in the social sciences, pointed to the Internet in particular as "allowing new forms of coordination of people, meetings, and events to emerge" (Sheller & Urry 2006, p.207). The Internet has created a technological endogeneity, an immanent world where everything is potentially connected to everything. Supporting this endogeneity is an infrastructure of wireless hotspots, cellphone base stations, and a variety of technological devices.

According to media scholar Adrian Mackenzie, this endogenous world is just another way of identifying the "naturalization" of Wi-Fi (Mackenzie 2005). "Wi-Fi," he writes, "has begun to 'naturalize' itself in buildings, cities, parks, transport systems, and towns throughout Europe, North America, Southeast Asia, Australia, and the Middle East" (Mackenzie 2005, p.269). In other words, Wi-Fi has, in some parts of the world, become simply part of the *environment*; it has become "invisible infrastructure"—that is, the "invisible work that affords the mobility of information (e.g., on the Internet)" (Mackenzie 2005, p.272). It is thought to "just be there." This is undoubtedly true at least in a city such as New York. Wi-Fi, while it was once only associated with coffee shops frequented by white, middle-class urbanites, is today even offered at McDonald's, airports, hotel lobbies, and bars among other places (Mackenzie 2005, p.278). Starbucks, in fact, as of 2010 July began to offer free Wi-Fi in all its US locations (Miller 2010). In Manhattan, this equates to a free wireless hotspot on nearly every corner.[1]

Wi-Fi (or "wireless fidelity") connects computers and devices through the Internet using radio links on a part of the radio spectrum—2.4/5 GHz—that is unlicensed. The transfer of information can occur over 200 feet (indoors) and 820 feet (outdoors). In addition, with cellular networks such as 3G and WiMax, there is an intensification of the Wi-Fi logic that Mackenzie looks at to even greater, more powerful connectivity. WiMax, for instance, provides speeds up to 40 Mbit/s, which is even greater than those of in-home, fiber optic (read: wired) Internet service packages that range from 15 Mbit/s to 50 Mbit/s. 3G and WiMax offer comparable Internet access and connectivity without the limitations of certain areas or zones as Wi-Fi hotspots are.

These developments, of course, affect everyday technological practice. As Mackenzie writes:

> ... [t]hese potentials induce people's movements in different bounded spaces (kitchens, lobbies, cabins, streets, offices, plazas, alleys, floors, gardens, filling station forecourts) connected to various movements of information (e-mailing, Webcam viewing, online chat, streaming audiovisual content such as music and TV, Internet telephony, blogging, photoblogging, online news, etc.).
>
> *(Mackenzie 2005, p.273)*

But, of course, this kind of multi-tasking can only be "induced," to use Mackenzie's word, if consumer devices are mobile and have Wi-Fi, 3G, or have some other form of networking capacity.

Thus we see that in the era of Web 2.0, consumer-level technological devices are designed to be portable and always Internet ready in some form or another. Take, for instance, the slew of ebook readers that are now on the market, the two most popular, at least in the USA, being the Amazon Kindle and the Apple iPad. The Kindle is an ebook reader that functions purely as that, with the added feature of being able to download books wirelessly through the Kindle store that is accessible through what Amazon calls Whispernet, which relies on a cellular carrier's network or Wi-Fi (Amazon n.d.). In its newest version, a battery charge supposedly lasts one month (Cellan-Jones 2010b). The Apple iPad functions, at least in terms of mobility and portability, in the same way. Although it is marketed as *more* than an ebook reader (in fact, the iPad seems to have created a new category of device that many media analysts are calling "tablets"), the iPad nevertheless shares the multiple options of Internet connectivity—3G and Wi-Fi. Although there are clear differences between how each of the devices is branded by its respective companies—the former stressing a single function while the latter its multi-functionality—they both exhibit the twin principles of portability and connectivity that characterize the devices of the invisible infrastructure of mobility.

The devices that grow out of the ecosystem of the contemporary wireless technostructure also lend to specific, "mobile" social media practices, the best example of which is "location tagging." Broadly speaking, location tagging consists of associating a location—through GPS coordinates, cellular base stations, or other means—with a message, a post or a particular file (usually a photo, in which case, the practice is call "geotagging"). Twitter and Facebook have their own versions of location tagging. In the case of the former, when the user enables geolocation, a Google Map appears, showing from where the tweet was sent. On Facebook, users are able to tag their location or "checkin," when they are using the mobile applications of Facebook. Both Twitter and Facebook, however, have only recently rolled out this location-tagging feature; they were mimicking Foursquare.

Although certainly not the first location-based social network, Foursquare is by far the most heavily used, certainly in the United States. Launched in 2009, Foursquare integrates with Twitter and Facebook, and "lets users 'check in' with a cellphone, at a bar, restaurant or art gallery. That alerts their friends to their current location so they can drop by and say hello." Part of its success is owed to its gaming aspects. "The system awards points and virtual badges to players depending on how often they go out and which places they visit. Users who frequent a particular place enough times are crowned 'mayor' of that particular location" (Wortham 2009). "Mayorship" seems to be the object of great investment by Foursquare users. As one *New York Times* article states:

> Even more baffling is why users have become so emotionally invested in being a mayor, as there are few, if any, tangible benefits. While some bars award free beer and some shops give small discounts as a marketing ploy, the majority do not.
>
> *(Oliver 2010)*

Foursquare embodies the blurring of the offline and the online that is at the heart of the techno-phenomenology of Web 2.0. That social networking *increases* "real-life" interactions was the mantra of many studies of early social networking. However, today, it is far less a debatable point. Location-based social networking such as Foursquare and the like herald a situation of "ubiquitous media" (Featherstone 2009), wherein Internet access can be carried with you. Just as broadband Internet killed the concept of "going online" in the days of dial-up by allowing users to always be online, mobile computing has completely eradicated the "online" as a distinct space or entity but rather has demonstrated the integrated nature of social media technologies today.

Spreadability

A fundamental consequence of the multi-tasking and mobility of Web 2.0 is that culture—as content or as information—becomes within reach all of a sudden. And true indeed, thus far, we have only addressed the *formal* aspects of the mobile experience of Web 2.0 but have not addressed the *content* of media. The formal interoperability that supports the mobile experience of Web 2.0 could not function without the "spreadability" of media content, as Henry Jenkins puts it (Jenkins et al. 2009).

Spreadability, for Jenkins et al., is a different way of approaching what some have called "viral" media" or "memes"—terms, which he believes "may be creating more confusion than clarity" due to their specifically biological origins (Jenkins et al. 2009). They fail to take into consideration the way in which media content is not only circulated, that is, forwarded, tweeted, and posted on one's Facebook status, but also "transformed, repurposed or distorted as they pass from hand to hand" (Jenkins et al. 2009). For Jenkins and his fellow researchers at the MIT Convergence Culture Consortium, the biological register of the "viral" and "meme" metaphors "promised a pseudo-scientific model for thinking about consumer behavior, one which kept power firmly in the hands of media producer . . . simply [mystifying] the process, limiting the industry's ability to understand the complex factors which now shape the creation of value through the circulation of content within these new social networks" (Jenkins et al. 2009). In other words, it is strictly the province of marketing and advertisers; it did very little analytically.

The framework of "spreadability" differs from the bio-analogous frameworks of media content primarily in the area of what Jenkins et al. call "media contact." Taking seriously O'Reilly's notion of the "architecture of participation," they argue that media content today moves "many-to-many" whereas existing models, such as "stickiness," treat the dynamic of media contact as primarily between the content media (a website, for instance) and the individual consumer. This, they call, "personalized media." At the core of "stickiness" is the idea that the measure of an individual's "investment," in particular content, can be measured by either time spent on a particular site visit or return visits. Jenkins et al. list Amazon or eBay as representing "the triumph" of the stickiness model as "both sites depend greatly on the return of highly committed and strongly motivated consumers and on multiple transactions per visit" (Jenkins et al. 2009). By way of contrast, "spreadability" hinges on the dispersal, not concentration. Instead of the user spending time looking at single piece of content (for instance, a Web ad), the idea would be to have the user *share* the content on his or her many social network accounts.

The best recent example of spreadable media has been a drinking game that took hold in parts of the United States among 20-something-year-olds called "icing." The game is predicated off an alcoholic malt beverage manufactured by Smirnoff called "Smirnoff Ice." It works like this. Someone (the "icer") presents a Smirnoff Ice to someone else. On seeing this, the recipient (the "icee") must get down on one knee, and drink the entire bottle unless he has a bottle of his own, in which case, the "icer" must drink *both*. The "purpose" is to avoid being "iced" since the drink is by all accounts terrible. For those who are unfamiliar with the product, the joke, which admittedly is not that funny, may be unclear. Among young Americans, Smirnoff Ice is seen as a "girly" drink, one that women would also object to if served it. Hence, to see mostly young, preppy white men getting down on one knee to chug such a drink is meant to portray a contradiction.

How "icing" came to be "the nation's biggest viral drinking game," as the *New York Times* describes it, is still somewhat of a mystery (Goodman 2010). According to many reports on the phenomenon "icing" first hit the Web en masse via a website called BrosIcingBros.com, which featured photos of various people drinking Smirnoff Ice while down on one knee. Much like the lolcat phenomenon associated with the blog I Can Has Cheezburger?, the website then slowly began to lose its central importance in headquartering "icing," with social networks such as Facebook and Twitter taking over for the sharing of "icing" photos and videos. It then took off to the point where people were getting "iced" at the workplace and family cookouts. The president of Princeton University even got iced. She declined (Saborio 2010). American political satirist Stephen Colbert even commented on the phenomenon.

Perhaps what is most remarkable about "icing" is that Smirnoff claims not only to be uninvolved with it but may have also had a hand in shutting down the BrosIcingBros.com website. In the parlance of Jenkins et al., it "spread," quite successfully, in spite of—or perhaps because of—the fact that Smirnoff had no idea who had started it and why it was popular. It was unlike the fantasy-oriented advertisements pioneered by the "Mad Men" of the 1960s, which required the viewer to identify with (or at least, aspire to) the character of the advertisement. "Icing" took off because it was participatory. The idea was to "ice" someone at your own workplace, at your own weekend cookout, document it and send it out to numerous social networks—on Tumblr, Twitter, Facebook, and YouTube.

This returns us to a point made throughout the course of this book: the traditional gap that used to exist between producer and audience has been somewhat bridged, albeit perhaps not entirely. In the case of "icing," the phenomena could only gain traction were it not for many people not only participating but also documenting and sharing it. This becomes easier due to certain features of social network sites as well as the "socialization" of software that has occurred, especially in the realm of media editing application such as Apple's iPhoto, which allows users to sync their photo collection with sites such as Flickr and Facebook. Micro-blogging services such as Tumblr and Posterous allow posting via email or apps allow for sharing on the move.

In terms of hardware, small cameras now too boast of direct upload to Facebook (Warren 2009), not to mention the fact that all smartphones today have cameras with an impressive number of megapixels and are, more so than cameras with wireless antennae, the most often used means of sharing photo and video content. Photos and short video clips now flood the feeds of Twitter and Facebook.

This is not to say that I view the overturning of the traditional relationship between producer and audience as the accomplishment of the Marxist hopes of the appropriation of the means of production from capital. This is far from the case. The media oligarchy in the United States, and, indeed, globally, is stronger than ever. What I am suggesting, however, is that there is a vast shift in the techno-phenomenological experience of computing in the era of Web 2.0. The ontological unit of the "cyborg" that dominated the discourse of technology studies in the 1990s is portrayed in artist Lynn Randolph's "Cyborg," which graces the cover of Haraway's *Simians, Cyborgs, and Women: The Reinvention of Nature.* It consists of a "woman of color with a large spirit-like feline draped atop her"(Haraway 1992) sitting—crucially—behind a keyboard. Perhaps a more apt illustration would be that of the "meanderthal:"

> A sort of human-variant, the Meanderthal could also be described as a Cyborg Spin-Off, exhibiting not only the machinic prosthetic appendages (e.g. cell-phone, BlackBerry) required of cyborg flesh, but also the sort of behavior—i.e. confusion, aimlessness, disorientation, self-absorption—that inevitably results when an all-too-human human attempts to navigate an overly mechanized and technologically-mediated environment. The technologically-induced distraction experienced by Meanderthals is compounded by their natural habitat—large, dense, heavily trafficked, urban environments. Indeed, the very systems they impede objectify their existence, for their own presence in the urban ecosystem is evident only to the degree to which they prevent the system in which they exist from functioning . . . They impede flows that are overdetermined, also, by the unrequited fantasy that the "meatscape"—the fleshly world—that inhabits the concrete caverns of the contemporary metropolis might become as fluid and efficient as the increasingly virtualized and immaterial economies of fiat currency thought to be the engines of urban and economic flows in the first place. The Meanderthal, then, is both product of and impediment to the technophilic and urbanized world we inhabit.
>
> *(Tiessen 2007)*

Note

1 In an ironic turn of events, high-end New York City coffee shops have begun to change their policies about free Wi-Fi, in attempts to decrease "laptop parking."

References

2010a. Britons "Multi-task' with Media, *BBC.* Available at: http://www.bbc.co.uk/news/technology-11012356. [Accessed August 21, 2010.]

2010b. multitasking, n. and adj. In *OED Online.* Available at: http://dictionary.oed.com.ezproxy.gc.cuny.edu/cgi/entry/00318370?query_type=word&queryword=

multi-task&first=1&max_to_show=10&sort_type=alpha&result_place=2. [Accessed August 21, 2010.]

Amazon, Amazon.com Help: Wireless, Whispernet, and Whispersync, *Amazon. com.* Available at: http://www.amazon.com/gp/help/customer/display. html?nodeId=200375890. [Accessed August 27, 2010.]

Anderson, C. & Wolff, M., 2010. The Web is Dead. Long Live the Internet, *Wired.* Available at: http://www.wired.com/magazine/2010/08/ff_webrip/all/1. [Accessed August 22, 2010.]

Bilton, N., 2010a. Bits Pics: Twitter Traffic During the World Cup, *Bits Blog.* Available at: http://bits.blogs.nytimes.com/2010/07/17/bits-pics-twitter-usage-during-the-world-cup/. [Accessed August 21, 2010.]

—— , 2010b. No E-Books Allowed in This Establishment, *Bits Blog.* Available at: http://bits.blogs.nytimes.com/2010/08/02/no-e-books-allowed-in-this-establishment/. [Accessed August 21, 2010.]

Buckley, C. & Richtel, M., 2010. Good Cellphone Service Comes at a Price, *New York Times.* Available at: http://www.nytimes.com/2010/08/21/nyregion/ 21celltower.html?_r=1&hp. [Accessed August 20, 2010.]

Cellan-Jones, R., 2010a. A Multi-tasking Moral Panic, *dot. Rory: A blog about technology.* Available at: http://www.bbc.co.uk/blogs/thereporters/rorycellanjones/2010/ 08/a_multi-tasking_moral_panic.html. [Accessed August 21, 2010.]

—— , 2010b. E-books: Amazon Bites Back, *dot. Rory: A blog about technology.* Available at: http://www.bbc.co.uk/blogs/thereporters/rorycellanjones/2010/07/ebooks_ amazon_bites_back.html. [Accessed August 27, 2010.]

Deleuze, G. & Guattari, F., 1987. *A Thousand Plateaus: Capitalism and Schizophrenia,* University of Minnesota Press.

Featherstone, M., 2009. Ubiquitous Media: An Introduction, *Theory, Culture & Society,* 26(2–3), 1.

Friedberg, A., 2006. *The Virtual Window: From Alberti to Microsoft,* MIT Press.

Galloway, A., 2007. 24/7, 16.8: Is 24 a Political Show?, *Afterimage,* 35(1), 18–22.

Goodman, J.D., 2010. Drinking Game Poses Query, Who's "Icing" Whom?, *New York Times.* Available at: http://www.nytimes.com/2010/06/09/business/ media/09adco.html?_r=1&ref=media. [Accessed August 28, 2010.]

Haraway, D., 1992. The Promises of Monsters, *Cultural Studies,* 295–337.

—— , 1990. *Simians, Cyborgs, and Women: The Reinvention of Nature* 1st edn, Routledge.

Howard, T., 2004. "Can You Hear Me Now?" A Hit, *USA Today.* Available at: http://www.usatoday.com/money/advertising/adtrack/2004-track-verizon_ x.htm. [Accessed August 20, 2010.]

Jenkins, H., Li, X., Domb Krauskopf, A., & Green, J. 2009. If It Doesn't Spread, It's Dead (Parts 1–8), *MIT Convergence Culture Consortium.* Available at: http://www. convergenceculture.org/weblog/2009/02/if_it_doesnt_spread_its_dead_p_7. php#more. [Accessed August 26, 2010.]

Lash, S., 2002. *Critique of Information* 1st edn, Sage.

Lohr, S., 2010. Now Playing: Night of the Living Tech, *New York Times.* Available at: http://www.nytimes.com/2010/08/22/weekinreview/22lohr.html?_r=1 [Accessed August 22, 2010.]

Mackenzie, A., 2005. Untangling the Unwired: Wi-Fi and the Cultural Inversion of Infrastructure, *Space and Culture*, 8(3), 269.

Manovich, L., 2007. *The Language of New Media*, MIT Press.

Miller, C.C., 2010. Starbucks to Offer Free Wi-Fi. *New York Times*. Available at: http://www.nytimes.com/2010/06/15/technology/15starbux. html?scp=1&sq=starbucks%20wifi&st=cse. [Accessed August 27, 2010.]

Oliver, S.S., 2010. Who Elected Me Mayor on Foursquare? I Did, *New York Times*. Available at: http://www.nytimes.com/2010/08/19/fashion/19foursquare. html?ref=technology. [Accessed August 27, 2010.]

Saborio, W., 2010. Breaking the Ice – "Shirley Tilghman: Not a Bro", *The Ink*. Available at: http://www.universitypressclub.com/archive/2010/06/one-ice-later-shirley-tilghman-not-a-bro/. [Accessed August 28, 2010.]

Sheller, M. & Urry, J., 2006. The New Mobilities Paradigm, *Environment and Planning A*, 38(2), 207.

Shiels, M., 2010. iPad to "Kickstart" Tablet Market. *BBC*. Available at: http://news.bbc.co.uk/2/hi/technology/8484395.stm. [Accessed August 21, 2010.]

Siegler, M., 2010. Just In Time For The Location Wars, Twitter Turns On Geolocation On Its Website, *TechCrunch*. Available at: http://techcrunch.com/2010/03/09/twitter-location-website/. [Accessed August 27, 2010.]

Slim, F., 2010. Guest Op Ed: Why Bros Get Iced, Bro, *The Awl*. Available at: http://www.theawl.com/2010/05/guest-op-ed-why-bros-get-iced-bro. [Accessed August 28, 2010.]

Stiegler, B., 2009. Teleologics of the Snail: The Errant Self Wired to a WiMax Network, *Theory, Culture & Society*, 26(2–3), 33.

Strand, O., 2010. The New Coffee Bars: Unplug, Drink Up, *New York Times*. Available at: http://www.nytimes.com/2010/08/25/dining/25coffee.html?_r=2&src=tptw. [Accessed August 28, 2010.]

Tiessen, M., 2007. Urban Meanderthals and the City of "Desire Lines," *CTheory.net*. Available at: http://www.ctheory.net/articles.aspx?id=583. [Accessed August 28, 2010.]

Vance, A. & Richtel, M., 2009. Light and Cheap, Netbooks Are Poised to Reshape PC Industry, *New York Times*. Available at: http://www.nytimes.com/2009/04/02/technology/02netbooks.html?_r=1&scp=3&sq=netbook&st=Search. [Accessed August 21, 2010.]

Warren, C., 2009. New Flip Video Camera Includes Direct Facebook Uploads, *Mashable*. Available at: http://mashable.com/2009/10/14/new-flip-video-camera-includes-direct-facebook-uploads/. [Accessed August 28, 2010.]

Wiener, N., 1965. *Cybernetics or Control and Communication in the Animal and the Machine*, MIT Press.

Wortham, J., 2009. Face-to-Face Socializing Starts With a Mobile Post, *New York Times*. Available at: http://www.nytimes.com/2009/10/19/technology/internet/19foursquare.html?ref=technology. [Accessed August 27, 2010.]

5

CRITICS OF WEB 2.0

Reading the informational politics of backlash

In November 2009 the *New York Times* Sunday Book Review published an essay entitled, "Is Technology Dumbing Down Japanese?" The article takes stock of the changes in the Japanese language as a result of media such as blogs and email but also "keitai shosetsu." As the article notes:

> Some of the most dramatic transformations have been taking place on cellphones, where writers, often young women, type stories into their keypads and readers consume them on their screens. Sentences tend to be short, and love stories are popular. The phenomenon peaked in 2007, when five out of 10 of the year's best-selling books were written on cellphones. While their popularity seems to have dropped off, keitai shosetsu still elicit scorn from some Japanese who see them as trashy.
>
> *(Parker 2009)*

What is important here is that while there has been no shortage of hostility towards the rising popularity of cellphone novels, especially by Minae Mizumura who contends that "the dominance of English, especially with the advent of the Internet, threatens to reduce all other national languages to mere 'local' languages that are not taken seriously by scholars," yet, as in the United States, the digitization of language has increased reading and writing. Critics have, in turn, questioned the *quality* of the reading and writing, wondering if reading the thoughts of friends on Facebook would count towards "reading" in this regard. This kind of reasoning is echoed in the much-talked-about article by Nicholas Carr entitled, "Is Google Making us Stupid?", which I discuss in greater detail in the following.

But, with the changes that have occurred in the nature of the World Wide Web, and the media-technological situation overall, a backlash is to be expected. It does not take much imagination to understand why. The increased visibility of Internet-related suicides, in addition to the already existing societal fear of sexual predators lurking on the Web (even inspiring an entire television series based on tracking down and shaming them), as well as the influx of identity fraud and phishing scams, not to mention the recent flare-ups about privacy issues on social networks, have made it hard for the Web to maintain the kind of image that it garnered during the dot-com boom as a utopian "information superhighway." Thus, the hype around Web 2.0 can be viewed as a strategic pushback against the recent stigma.

Therefore, it is no surprise that, in the wake of Web 2.0, the backlash to Web 2.0 has recently picked up great momentum among intellectuals, media pundits, and others, resulting in a slew of blog posts, magazine articles, and books critiquing its core principles of participation, decentralization, and democratization. And, in this chapter, we will reckon with some of the voices of skepticism.

Surprisingly, these voices of skepticism have not come from the same intellectual or political position; they represent rather varied ones. In my view, we can constructively analyze the discourse of the backlash by breaking it down into three distinct currents: (1) Critics, such as computer scientist Jaron Lanier and technology writer Nicholas Carr, have specifically taken on the task of retorting the digital behaviorism of those like Chris Anderson and Kevin Kelly. The titles of their recent books in this regard make this much clear—*You Are Not a Gadget: A Manifesto* (Lanier) and *The Shallows: How the Internet is Changing the Way We Think, Read and Remember* (Carr). (2) Others, like Andrew Keen, have argued that Web 2.0 has given rise to a culture of amateurism, which threatens western civilization at its core. (3) And some, like Dutch net critic Geert Lovink, mentioned earlier, have criticized Web 2.0 from the political left, suggesting that it is not as democratic and participatory as advertised. Although flawed and perhaps oversimplified, this typology will guide us through the discourse that has been highly critical of Web 2.0, especially in analyzing the informational politics of the backlash.

What are "informational politics"? Although a detailed discussion of the term would require more space than this chapter provides and has been attempted elsewhere, informational politics refer to the fact that politics are not outside of the realm of technologies; they are, rather, intrinsic to them, that is to say, certain structural, technical and/or architectural aspects of the software or website have certain political implications. Media theorist Alex Galloway, in his *Protocol*, has most forcefully articulated this point:

> Perhaps it is a different type of control than we are used to seeing. It is a type of control based on openness, inclusion, universalism, and flexibility. It is a type of control borne from high degrees of technical organization (protocol), not this or that limitation on individual freedom or decision making (fascism).
>
> *(Galloway 2004, p.142)*

Just as Galloway does with regard to the informational politics of the Internet, we can also view Web 2.0 in a similar way, that is, through the prism of its implicit politics.

Non-neutral critique

We will begin with an analysis of (1), which I label the *non-neutral* critique, of which the representative figures are Lanier and Carr, whose respective works have garnered a significant amount of attention within and outside of technologist circles. By non-neutral, I mean to suggest that both Lanier and Carr view technology as having actual effects on human beings. The Web is not simply a tool for human use but, in this view, it has lasting effects on what it *means* to be human. This is a view that, in the western tradition of philosophy at least, begins with Heidegger, although perhaps the abstract notion of "Dasein" is not exactly at the forefront of Lanier and Carr's intellectual concerns. It is clear that their main frame of reference is McLuhan.

Carr's article "Is Google Making Us Stupid?" appeared in *The Atlantic* to much critical attention, thanks in large part to the sensationalist title. The article was not so much about Google making people stupid but rather a broad-stroked exploration of the effects of ubiquitous media and the increase in time spent on the Internet.

For the most part, there was not much in the form of new research or new perspective with regard to the effect of computing on the brain. Instead, in a fashion similar to that of Malcolm Gladwell, Carr brought together neurological and psychological research to argue that the World Wide Web "[shapes] the process of thought." As Carr describes it:

> And what the Net seems to be doing is chipping away my capacity for concentration and contemplation. My mind now expects to take in information the way the Net distributes it: in a swiftly moving stream of particles. Once I was a scuba diver in the sea of words. Now I zip along the surface like a guy on a Jet Ski.
>
> . . .
>
> I can feel it most strongly when I'm reading. Immersing myself in a book or a lengthy article used to be easy. My mind would get caught up in the narrative or the turns of the argument, and I'd spend hours strolling through long stretches of prose. That's rarely the case anymore. Now my concentration often starts to drift after two or three pages. I get fidgety, lose the thread, begin looking for something else to do. I feel as if I'm always dragging my wayward brain back to the text. The deep reading that used to come naturally has become a struggle.
>
> *(N. Carr 2008)*

This, Carr suggests, is symptomatic of the "staccato"-style of reading and, more broadly, thinking of the Web. Blog posts, tweets, status updates— the forms of writing that are prevalent on Web 2.0 are short.

> When we go online, we enter an environment that promotes cursory reading, hurried and distracted thinking, and superficial learning. Even as the Internet grants us easy access to vast amounts of information, it is turning us into shallower thinkers, literally changing the structure of our brain.
>
> *(N. Carr 2010)*

Reading has a particularly privileged place in Carr's overall argument about how the Web affects us. He argues that "media or other technologies we use in learning and practicing the craft of reading play an important part in shaping the neural circuits inside our brains," citing "experiments [that] demonstrate that readers of ideograms, such as the Chinese, develop a mental circuitry for reading that is very different from the circuitry found in those of us whose written language employs an alphabet" (N. Carr 2008).

As he suggests, the Web has made a specific mode of reading more conducive than others. This mode consists mostly of skimming and "light reading." This is especially the case with many Web articles and blog posts including hyperlinks—links to other content on the Web. This speaks to the difficulty of staying in "one place," so to speak, especially as all the major Web browsers—Firefox, Internet Explorer, Safari, Chrome—feature multiple-tab browsing, allowing for the user to have several pages open at the same time. Further, with services that cull RSS feeds such as Google Reader allow for users to have instant access to a large amount of content, particularly text, in one "web space." As Carr writes:

> Thanks to the ubiquity of text on the Internet, not to mention the popularity of text-messaging on cell phones, we may well be reading more today than we did in the 1970s or 1980s, when television was our medium of choice. But it's a different kind of reading, and behind it lies a different kind of thinking—perhaps even a new sense of the self.
>
> *(N. Carr 2008)*

Reading, as Carr points out, becomes lighter, that is to say, "our ability to interpret text, to make the rich mental connections that form when we read deeply and without distraction, remains largely disengaged" (N. Carr 2008).

In light of these design specificities of navigating the Web, the non-linear mode of reading on the Web poses a psychological and neurological change in humans. "The distinctive neural pathways of experienced Web users," he writes, "had developed because of their Internet use" (N. Carr 2010). Brains, he argues, are malleable, plastic, citing current research that shows that "our mental meshwork, the dense connections formed among the 100 billion or so neurons inside our skulls" is not fixed by adulthood (N. Carr 2008). To the contrary, "the human brain is highly plastic; neurons and synapses change as circumstances change" (N. Carr 2010).

According to researchers like Erping Zhu, reading comprehension declines "as the number of links increased—whether or not people clicked on them." This means that the brain is distracted when there is no clicking of the link, since it must decided whether to do so or not. What occurs, then, when reading something riddled with hyperlinks, is an overflow of the cognitive load, that is, information runs over the threshold under which the human mind can process and store information. "We can't translate the new material into conceptual knowledge," as Carr describes it. There is a high "switching cost," a term used by brain scientists to refer to what happens when we shift our attention and "the brain has to reorient itself, further taxing our mental resources" (N. Carr 2010).

Ultimately, for Carr, this is not necessarily a bad thing. Some cognitive effects of the World Wide Web strengthen certain functions of the brain with regard to problem solving and spotting patterns in data. The "discretization" of data has been around since newspapers and, of course, the advent of papers such as *USA Today* as well as newswire services such as the Associated Press. However, the negatives, in this argument, outweigh the positives, the biggest being what Carr rather dramatically describes as the weakening of reflection, that is, "deep thinking" that results from sustained engagement with long pieces of writing. It becomes problematic when, as he says, "skimming becomes the *dominant* mode of thought," the consequences of which affect "our intellectual lives and even our culture." He concludes: "We are evolving from cultivators of personal knowledge into hunters and gatherers in the electronic data forest. In the process, we seem fated to sacrifice much of what makes our minds so interesting" (N. Carr 2010).

In a similar vein, Jaron Lanier, a computer scientist who is responsible for the term "virtual reality," surprised many who know of his reputation, when he came out with a self-described manifesto against the slide towards the eradication of what he calls "human specialness." Beginning with an essay that appeared on the online magazine *Edge* called "Digital Maoism: The Hazards of the New Online Collectivism," which figured prominently in his subsequent book *You Are Not a Gadget*, and most recently in a widely circulated essay entitled "The End of Human Specialness," Lanier has become the major *humanist* critic of not only Web 2.0 but what he considers the *ideology* of Web 2.0—"computationalism." "This ideology," he writes, "promotes radical freedom on the surface of the Web, but that freedom, ironically, is more for machines than people. Nevertheless, it is sometimes referred to as 'open culture' " (Lanier 2010b, p.3).

This ideology, argues Lanier, has spread like a virus and has affected not only culture but also the very nature of what it means to be human, which for him, is undoubtedly "special," a term which he uses time and time again. What is to be meant by it? Is it the Christian doctrine of *imago Dei* in which Augustine locates human reason or that of Adamic dominion over the rest of creation? No. (Lanier saves choice words for religion and in fact accuses the ideology of Web 2.0 of being a religion.) The "human" at the heart of Lanier's critique is that of Enlightenment humanism—the individual.

More specifically, Lanier views the ideology of Web 2.0 to be what he calls "digital Maoism" or "cybernetic totalism" which forces, through software design and architecture, a collectivity that dissolves "the belief in the self" (Lanier 2010a). He argues:

> The central mistake of recent digital culture is to chop up a network of individuals so finely that you end up with a mush. You then start to care about the abstraction of the network more than the real people who are networked, even though the network by itself is meaningless. Only the people were ever meaningful.
>
> *(Lanier 2010b, p.17)*

"The deep meaning of personhood," he writes, "is being reduced by illusions of bits" (Lanier 2010b, p.20). This is great writing to be sure, but does the argument have merit? Is Lanier right?

According to this argument, the main thinkers behind this ideology of antihuman computationalism are the gurus of Web 2.0, in particular Chris Anderson and Kevin Kelly, who are affiliated with *Wired* magazine. They celebrate Wikipedia and other forms of open source uncritically, praising the collective without fully reckoning with the consequences of their views. It breeds, Lanier argues:

> a new online collectivism that is nothing less than a resurgence of the idea that the collective is all-wise, that it is desirable to have

influence concentrated in a bottleneck that can channel the collective with the most verity and force. This is different from representative democracy, or meritocracy.

(Lanier 2006)

The hype around Wikipedia, according to Lanier, wreaks of an ideological computationalism that views all reality as information. It reflects "the Oracle illusion, in which knowledge of the human authorship of a text is suppressed in order to give the text superhuman validity" (Lanier 2010b, p.32). It treats Wikipedia as a living entity on the same plane, if not *above*, humans. This is also operant in the attention recently being paid to ideas such as "crowdsourcing."

For Lanier, this leads to disastrous consequences, as the collective is automatically assumed to be not only correct but also more important than the individual:

The attribution of intelligence to machines, crowds of fragments, or other nerd deities obscures more than it illuminates. When people are told that a computer is intelligent, they become prone to changing themselves in order to make the computer appear to work better, instead of demanding that the computer be changed to become more useful. People already tend to defer to computers, blaming themselves when a digital gadget or online service is hard to use.

(Lanier 2010b, p.36)

To be fair, he does admit that there are times when the collective works well and does not result in the devaluation of personhood. Tellingly, an example that he gives of this is that of market capitalism, going so far as to call Adam Smith's notion of the invisible hand "clever." He favorably refers to this as "blind elitism," that is, "blind in the sense that ideally anyone can gain entry, but only on the basis of a meritocracy" (Lanier 2006).

Here, we see that Lanier is not only reproducing the simplest of neo-liberal ideology, but uncritically placing contemporary capitalism and democracy as an ideal social framework. In other words, the regulations that currently create a certain degree of elitism work to ensure expertise and true wisdom, as he sees it. As he writes:

The calming effect of orderly democracy achieves more than just smoothing out of peripatetic struggles for consensus. It also reduces the potential for the collective to suddenly jump into an over-excited state when too many rapid changes to answers coincide in such a way that they don't cancel each other out.

(Lanier 2006)

Blind elitism protects against the "fascist," or "totalitarian," *design* of the user interface of the Web, leading to "negative patterns of behavior or even bring about unforeseen social pathology" (Lanier 2010b, p.64). This includes not only illegal consumption and circulation of various media, especially music and film, but also software through a file-sharing protocol like BitTorrent. Further, the practice of creating a profile in social networks such as Facebook, Lanier suggests, is an exercise in "personal reductionism."

You fill in the data: profession, marital status, and residence. But in this case digital reduction becomes a causal element, mediating contact between new friends. That is new. It used to be that government was famous for being impersonal, but in a postpersonal world, that will no longer be a distinction.

(Lanier 2010b, p.69)

Facebook, then, is an example of what Lanier refers to as the "behavioral failure" of computationalism, the reigning ideology of technology in the era of Web 2.0, wherein "people . . . make themselves believe in all sorts of fictitious beings, [which] are perceived as inhabiting the software tools through which we live our lives, we [end up changing] ourselves in unfortunate ways in order to support our fantasies." The recursive loop of humans making technologies which then reflects back onto humanity's self-imaging of human nature in technological terms confines "humanity" to a specific technological regime. The result is, as he says, "we make ourselves dull" (Lanier 2010b, p.157). Evoking the language of monopolies, Lanier refers to this situation as "lock-in." We are locked into a view of technologies as persons and persons as technologies.

The respective critiques of Lanier and Carr constitute a curious intellectual position. They are undoubtedly anti-Web 2.0 but have a decidedly pro-ontological, or "non-neutral" theory of technology (Feenberg 1991), harkening to a position articulated by Jacques Ellul, the French critic of technology, who wrote:

> ... [W]hen technique enters into every area of life, including the human, it ceases to be external to man and becomes his very substance. It is no longer face to face with man but is integrated with him, and it progressively absorbs him.
>
> *(Ellul 1964, p.6)*

The elitist critique

Andrew Keen, the self-professed Silicon Valley insider/entrepreneur turned Web 2.0 critic, has a position similar to that of the non-neutral critique of Lanier and Carr but with a large dose of elitism. Like Lanier and Carr, he is unequivocally *against* Web 2.0. Unlike them, however, Keen's position tends not to focus on the effect of technologies on human behavior, that is, on neurology or psychology but on their effect on "western culture," specifically the tenets of the Enlightenment. In *The Cult of the Amateur*, a book that has garnered its fair share of praise and disagreement, Keen writes:

> I believe it lies at the heart of Web 2.0's cultural revolution and threatens to turn our intellectual traditions and institutions upside down. In one sense, representing the triumph of innocence over experience, of romanticism over the commonsense wisdom of the Enlightenment.
>
> *(Keen 2007, p.36)*

Interestingly, he never fully articulates what he means by the Enlightenment, and is utterly unaware, or at least seems to leave unacknowledged, that the intellectual and cultural inheritance of the Enlightenment has been a subject of debate in many disciplines. Thus, throughout the course of his book, the Enlightenment becomes reified and, in turn, used as a "straw man," although not in the traditional sense of mischaracterizing one's opponent's rationale or argument. In this instance, Keen's "Enlightenment" is a straw man that he mischaracterizes for the sake of his argument. This becomes especially clear when Keen, while, on the one hand, defending the Enlightenment, writes against the democratization that he describes to be at heart of Web 2.0, on the other. In fact, one could replace Keen's original subtitle for his book from "How Today's Internet is Killing Our Culture" to "What Happens When There is Too Much Democracy."

While the title of his book may suggest that Keen's main object of contempt is "the amateur," it is indeed the overturning of specific power relations of a pre-World Wide Web time, which he, undoubtedly drawing from Thomas Friedman (2005), calls "flattening." For Keen, the "flattening" that blurs the line between "traditional audience and author, creator and consumer, expert and amateur" has "seduced" so many, taking hold of the public imagination. "This," he writes, "is no laughing matter" (Keen 2007, p.2).

According to Keen, the great seduction of Web 2.0, in large part, has to do with the peddled "promise of bringing more truth to more people— more depth of information, more global perspective, more unbiased opinion from dispassionate observers. But this is all a smokescreen."

> What the Web 2.0 revolution is really delivering is superficial observations of the world around us rather than deep analysis, shrill opinion rather than considered judgment. The information business is being transformed by the Internet into the sheer noise of a hundred million bloggers all simultaneously talking about themselves.
>
> *(Keen 2007, p.16)*

Echoing the sentiments of Carr regarding the end of reflection in particular ("shrill opinion rather than considered judgment"), Keen here is partaking in a moral critique of Web 2.0. The widespread democratization of Web 2.0 has resulted in not only a new type of knowledge formation but also a viral narcissism, a hyper-individualized network of people, not a community. Keen again:

> This infinite desire for personal attention is driving the hottest part of the new Internet economy—social-networking sites like MySpace, Facebook, and Bebo. As shrines for the cult of self-broadcasting, these sites have become tabula rasas of our individual desires and

identities. They claim to be all about "social networking" with others, but in reality they exist so that we can advertise ourselves: everything from our favorite books and movies, to photos from our summer vacations, to "testimonials" praising our more winsome qualities or recapping our latest drunken exploits. It's hardly surprising that the increasingly tasteless nature of such self-advertisements has led to an infestation of anonymous sexual predators and pedophiles.

(Keen 2007, p.7)

The moral critique that Keen attempts wears thin very quickly as he links pedophilia to self-broadcasting. While undoubtedly sexual predators on the World Wide Web is not something to take lightly, Keen here, by correlating Internet-facilitated "amateurism" to sex crimes, engages in more than a bit of intellectual dishonesty.

The amateur, the viral narcissist who thinks he can and should deserve the same notoriety and respect as traditional media institutions, functions as the embodiment of all that is wrong with the Web 2.0 "revolution." The amateur blogger has replaced the seasoned (and credentialed journalist.) The YouTube star has replaced the Hollywood film director and actor. The Flickrer and Tumblerer have replaced the professional photographer. Web 2.0 is slowly replacing the institutions of mainstream media, such as newspapers and broadcast news, he suggests:

The monkeys take over. Say good-bye to today's experts and cultural gatekeepers—our reporters, news anchors, editors, music companies, and Hollywood movie studios.

(Keen 2007, p.9)

But Keen has something very specific in mind when he is bemoaning the debasement of western culture (globalization rather conveniently does not factor in his account). He is talking about the reorientation of power dynamics that had held up the professional media industries in the past, which have, in his mind, structured a healthy civic culture. Therefore, he is able to write, it is "the decline of the quality and reliability of the information we receive, thereby distorting, if not outrightly corrupting, our national civic conversation" (Keen 2007, p.27). Harkening to arguments made by social scientists in the 1970s regarding the "culture of narcissism" (Lasch 1991), he argues that the amateur of Web 2.0 has "threatened" civic discourse.

As an example, he points to YouTube's effect on electoral politics. For Keen, the "YouTubification" of politics "silences public discourse" and "infantilizes the political process," allowing short video clips to take down political careers. As an illustration, he rather confusingly points to an incident that occurred with a former US Senator from Virginia, George Allen, who, on the campaign trail in 2006, used a racist epithet to refer to a campaign staffer of his opponent who had been following the campaign around with a camcorder. The entire episode, where Allen refers to the staffer, an Indian-American born in Virginia, as "macaca," a racist term often used by Francophone colonialists to refer to the darker skinned people of the Congo and North Africa, was recorded and uploaded to YouTube. The video clip derailed Allen's campaign as it picked up steam on YouTube, ultimately making it to mainstream news outlets (Craig & Shear 2006). Indeed, the staffer to whom the slur was directed was hired by Allen's opponent to record all of Allen's campaign stump speeches. But it still does not explain, at least for me, why Keen writes as if Allen were a victim of the culture of the YouTubification of politics and views. This example, for him, is an example of the civility threatened, as opposed to racism.

The solution to the Web 2.0 problem, for Keen, is simple. It is:

> to protect the legacy of our mainstream media and two hundred years of copyright protections within the context of twenty-first-century digital technology. Our goal should be to preserve our culture and our values, while enjoying the benefits of today's Internet capabilities. We need to find a way to balance the best of the digital future without destroying the institutions of the past.
>
> *(Keen 2007, p.185)*

Here, we see most plainly, the brand of elitism of Keen. It is an elitism that is rooted a defensive position against the slow debasement of "culture" or "civilization" or "tradition." It is the elitism of Mosca and Ortega y Gasset (Gasset 1994; Mosca 1960). Or better yet, that of Matthew Arnold, who famously defined culture as "the best that has been thought and said in the world" (Arnold 1960, p.6). It is one that equates culture and values to institutions such as the mainstream media, of the expert. Wittingly or not, we see that Keen is articulating an anti-Web 2.0 argument based on the defense of large, privately owned media companies. Although he would not put it this way, one could venture to suggest Keen's argument to be pro-capitalist, anti-democratic. He concludes:

> Instead of developing technology, I believe that our real moral responsibility is to protect mainstream media against the cult of the amateur. We need to reform rather than revolutionize an information and entertainment economy that, over the last two hundred years, has reinforced American values and made our culture the envy of the world.
>
> *(Keen 2007, p.204)*

Keen's argument raises several questions. For instance, why is it that western culture in its entirety is equated with the likes of Rupert Murdoch's NewsCorp, of which the *Wall Street Journal* is a subsidiary? Further, why is the media landscape a zero-sum game? Are the pre-Web 2.0 power dynamics in contemporary American society all that great so as to tout what has followed in the wake of Web 2.0 an utter civilizational disaster, as Keen has?

If one looks at the run up to Operation Iraqi Freedom (otherwise known as the Iraq War), we see that the traditional news media, in which Keen has so much faith, failed to question the accuracy of the intelligence linking 9/11 and the repressive regime of Saddam Hussein. As Jay Rosen, press critic and convenor of the blog PressThink, rightly notes:

> When (with some exceptions) political journalists failed properly to examine George W. Bush's case for war in Iraq, they were making a category mistake. They treated Bush's plan as part of the sphere of consensus. But even when Congress supports it, a case for war can never be removed from legitimate debate. That's just a bad idea. Mentally placing the war's opponents in the sphere of deviance was another category error. In politics, when people screw up like that, we can replace them: *throw the bums out!* we say. But the First Amendment says we cannot do that to people in the press. The bums stay. And later they are free to say: we didn't screw up at

all, as David Gregory, now host of Meet the Press, did say to his
enduring shame.

(Rosen 2009)

Mainstream news media, with its traditional authority, was able to dictate
what was considered "legitimate" or not in the press coverage leading up
to the invasion of Iraq. In hindsight, we see that this had disastrous consequences for assessing Keen's argument. In this instance at least, the elite,
in fact, failed to do what Keen suggests they do best.

The leftist critique

In the previous chapters, we have encountered the work of Geert Lovink.
His critique on Web 2.0 differs radically from that of the non-neutral
critique of Lanier and Carr as well as the elitist critique of Keen. In
an article that first appeared in the Net-time mailing list and later
reprinted in a variety of online forums entitled "The Digital Given: 10
Web 2.0 Theses," Lovink, along with the Italian collective Ippolita
and Australian media theorist Ned Rossiter, set off an intellectual
earthquake among leftist media theory circles. It was a line in the sand,
separating what they believed to be the hype from the reality. Like others,
the intellectual and cultural left in the west had largely viewed Web 2.0
as democratization of some sort. The increased participatory nature
of social media, for instance, created a sense of more democratic or
participatory politics. But for Lovink et al., Web 2.0 was not democratic
enough.

While this may sound like a far cry from the positions of both the non-
neutral camp and the elitist camp, there are, surprisingly, many points of
commonality between the leftist critique and the others just mentioned.
For one, Lovink et al. view Web 2.0 technologies, in particular social
networks, to be those of mere "entertainment and diffusion" (Lovink et al.
2009). As they argue:

> We initially love them for their distraction from the torture of
> now-time. Networking sites are social drugs for those in need of the
> Human that is located else wherein time or space. It is the pseudo
> Other that we are connecting to. Not the radical Other or some real

Other. We systematically explore weakness and vagueness and are
pressed to further enhance the exhibition of the Self.

(Lovink et al. 2009)

In much the same way as Keen, they suggest that Web 2.0's core logic is
that of narcissism. Thus for them, the "social" of "social media" is insuf-
ficient. "What the online world needs is sustainable social relations," they
write. "The moving herds of that go from one server to the next merely
demonstrate an impulsive grazing mentality: once the latest widgets are
installed, it is time to move on." It is the temporary nature of sociality of
Web 2.0 with which Lovink et al. have the most problem. The weakness of
social media, they argue, is "their seeming incapacity to effect political
change in any substantive way." A propos to the concerns of this chapter,
they cite the example of citizen-journalism:

The valorisation of citizen-journalism is not the same as radical
intervention, and is better understood as symptomatic of the structural logic of outsourcing media production and election campaign
management.

(Lovink et al. 2009)

Their quasi-Marxist interpretation of the phenomena of citizen journalism
demonstrates not only their skepticism but also their dissatisfaction. While
for Keen ordinary citizens taking to Twitter and YouTube signals a tidal
wave of revolution of the amateur, for Lovink et al. it is merely another
instance of exploitation in the broadest, and perhaps crude, sense. "From
social to socialism is a small step for humankind—but a big step for the
western subject," they insist.

And indeed, social media do not equate to socialism, the debates on
"online collectivism" (discussed in Chapter 3) notwithstanding. Social
media, while they may pique the imagination and hint at some kind of
process of democratization or great participation, have, in reality, not
transformed concrete conditions:

Tag, Connect, Friend, Link, Share, Tweet. These are not terms that
signal any form of collective intelligence, creativity or networked
socialism. They are directives from the Central Software Committee.

"Participation" in "social networks" will no longer work, if it ever did, as the magic recipe to transform tired and boring individuals into cool members of the mythological Collective Intelligence. If you're not an interesting individual, your participation is not really interesting. Data clouds, after all, are clouds: they fade away.

(Lovink et al. 2009)

Taking direct aim at the term "collective intelligence," coined by media theorist Pierre Levy and heralded by Tim O'Reilly, Lovink et al. suggest that the social technologies of Web 2.0 do not form any semblance of such.

Their critique has two aspects. On the one hand, they suggest that the sociality of Web 2.0 depends on corporate technologies. The design, structure, and availability of these technologies are all at the mercy of companies who do not have any sort of interest in "socialism" or the like. They are more worried about the latest wave of funding and buyout offers than politics. To be sure, Lovink et al. are correct on this point. On the other hand, they continue to bemoan the temporary nature of the new wave of social technologies. They are unconvinced of its lasting promise. They have very little faith that Web 2.0 will form lasting *institutions*.

Although they do not say so in this particular manifesto, the authors are no doubt "institutionalists" politically. That is to say, they believe that a truly left, digital politics of the proper order needs to work to "invent new institutional forms," which is the subtitle of Rossiter's website (Rossiter 2008). Hence, Lovink et al. suggest that one of the major drawbacks of social networks to be the softening of antagonism, that is, the end of negation. Harkening back to a central concern of the Frankfurt School thinkers, but perhaps most identifiable in the work of Herbert Marcuse, Lovink et al. complain: "Where is the enemy? Not on Facebook, where you can only have 'friends.' What Web 2.0 lacks is the technique of antagonistic linkage. Instead, we are confronted with the Tyranny of Positive Energy" (Lovink et al. 2009).

Here again, we see the true colors of Lovink et al. as "critical Marxists." Although freed from the "vulgar" orthodoxy of Marxist eschatology, the authors offer a critique of Web 2.0 that, in sum, suggests that it is not "free" although it may be open. There is a cost to Web 2.0:

> We need to question naive campaigns that merely promote "free culture" without questioning the underlying parasitic economy and the "deprofessionalization" of cultural work. Pervasive profiling is the cost of this opening to "free market values." As users and prosumers we are limited by our capacity as data producers. Our tastes and preferences, our opinions and movements are the market price to pay.
>
> *(Lovink et al. 2009)*

Here, they are pointing to the practice of data mining, wherein one's browsing activity is tracked in order to target advertisements more effectively (Helft & Vega 2010) in order to suggest that even net time is labor time.

So Lovink, Ippolita and Rossiter make up a "leftist" critique of Web 2.0, which, while it shares some of the concerns of both the non-neutral and elitist critique, is one that believes Keen, Carr and Lanier are *overstating* the revolutionary nature of Web 2.0. While they acknowledge that the influence of Web 2.0 is nothing to scoff at, because they are indeed scholars of the Internet, they do not see Web 2.0 nearly as democratic and participatory as perhaps the most vocal of backlashers like Keen.

Is it all hype?

With the wide-ranging critiques as well as proclamations of its death having now appeared (Anderson & Wolff 2010), the question thus lingers: is Web 2.0 mostly hype generated by specific media elites? The answer, admittedly unsatisfying, is that maybe it is and maybe it isn't. While there is no doubt that Web 2.0 as a phenomenon has been a product of a collusion between a specific technological ideology and business interests, there is no reason to deny that tenets associated with it have become so entrenched that even Lovink et al. consider it a part of "the digital given."

For that reason, David Carr, media critic for the *New York Times* (and no relation to Nicholas), proclaims, "Twitter will endure" because it has become "plumbing" (D. Carr 2010). Like plumbing, the barrier for entry is quite low and convenient. Twitter is so "friction free," as he describes it. Unlike Facebook, which relies on a "gift economy" of social expectations, Twitter allows the user to "forget that others are out there listening." Carr writes:

At first, Twitter can be overwhelming, but think of it as a river of data rushing past that I dip a cup into every once in a while. Much of what I need to know is in that cup: if it looks like Apple is going to demo its new tablet, or Amazon sold more Kindles than actual books at Christmas, or the final vote in the Senate gets locked in on health care, I almost always learn about it first on Twitter.

(D. Carr 2010)

It becomes, for Carr, a means by which to listen to a "wired collective voice." Its use-value comes from the possibility of "practical magic," a term he uses to describe the use of Twitter as a feedback mechanism for things such as flight delays:

But in the right circumstance, Twitter can flex some big muscles. Think of last weekend, a heavy travel period marked by a terrorist incident on Friday. As news outlets were scrambling to understand the implications for travelers on Saturday morning, Twitter began lighting up with reports of new security initiatives, including one from @CharleneLi, a consultant who tweeted from the Montreal airport at about 7:30 a.m.: "New security rules for int'l flights into US. 1 bag, no electronics the ENTIRE flight, no getting up last hour of flight."

(D. Carr 2010)

What Carr's anecdote reveals is not so much "Look how useful Twitter can be" because along with helpful information such as that just cited, there are plenty of "I just ate a bowl of cereal" tweets as well. But this is beside the point. What Carr's example of Twitter demonstrates most accurately is *how* media technologies are used in the era of Web 2.0 but easily it is integrated into the "mobile lives" (Elliott & Urry 2010) of many in the world today.

While it will continue to be the subject of debates regarding its use-value as a periodization term or as an actually existing collection of principles, Web 2.0 is already here. Oddly enough, this is what nearly all critical positions of Web 2.0 seem to agree on. The conditions by which we use World Wide Web today—the multi-functionality of technological devices and its correlative mobile computing experience, the proliferation of user-generated content such as blogging and the correspondent over-turning of the relationship of producer and consumer and the new forms of sociality characteristic of Web 2.0—are foundational.

References

2007. Facebook "Costs Businesses Dear", *BBC*. Available at: http://news.bbc.co.uk/2/hi/6989100.stm. [Accessed September 9, 2010.]

Anderson, C. & Wolff, M., 2010. The Web is Dead. Long Live the Internet, *Wired*. Available at: http://www.wired.com/magazine/2010/08/ff_webrip/all/1. [Accessed August 22, 2010.]

Arnold, M., 1960. *Culture and Anarchy* (J. D. Wilson, ed.), Cambridge University Press.

Carr, D., 2010. Why Twitter Will Endure, *New York Times*. Available at: http://www.nytimes.com/2010/01/03/weekinreview/03carr.html. [Accessed September 9, 2010.]

Carr, N., 2008. Is Google Making Us Stupid?, *The Atlantic* (July/August). Available at: http://www.theatlantic.com/magazine/archive/2008/07/is-google-making-us-stupid/6868/. [Accessed September 3, 2010.]

—— , 2010a. *The Shallows: How the Internet Is Changing the Way We Think, Read and Remember*, Atlantic Books.

—— , 2010b. The Web Shatters Focus, Rewires Brains, *Wired*, 18(09). Available at: http://www.wired.com/magazine/2010/05/ff_nicholas_carr/all/1. [Accessed September 5, 2010.]

Craig, T. & Shear, M., 2006. Allen Quip Provokes Outrage, Apology, *Washington Post*. Available at: http://www.washingtonpost.com/wp-dyn/content/article/2006/08/14/AR2006081400589.html. [Accessed September 8, 2010.]

Elliott, A. & Urry, J., 2010. *Mobile Lives*, Routledge.

Ellul, J., 1964. *The Technological Society*, Vintage Books.

Feenberg, A., 1991. *Critical Theory of Technology*, Oxford University Press.

Friedman, T.L., 2005. *The World Is Flat: A Brief History of the Twenty-first Century* 1st edn, Farrar, Straus & Giroux.

Galloway, A.R., 2004. *Protocol*, MIT Press.

Gasset, J.O.Y., 1994. *The Revolt of the Masses*, W. W. Norton & Company.

Han, S., 2007. *Navigating Technomedia: Caught in the Web*, Rowman & Littlefield.

Helft, M. & Vega, T., 2010. Retargeting Ads Follow Surfers to Other Sites, *New York Times*. Available at: http://www.nytimes.com/2010/08/30/technology/30adstalk.html?_r=1. [Accessed September 9, 2010.]

Keen, A., 2007. *The Cult of the Amateur: How Today's Internet is Killing Our Culture*, Crown Business.

Lanier, J., 2010a. The End of Human Specialness, *The Chronicle of Higher Education*. Available at: http://chronicle.com/article/article-content/124124/. [Accessed September 4, 2010.]

—— , 2010b. *You Are Not a Gadget: A Manifesto* 1st edn, Knopf.

——, 2006. DIGITAL MAOISM: The Hazards of the New Online Collectivism, *Edge: The Third Culture*. Available at: http://www.edge.org/3rd_culture/lanier06/lanier06_index.html. [Accessed September 4, 2010.]

Lasch, C., 1991. *The Culture of Narcissism: American Life in an Age of Diminishing Expectations* rev. edn, W. W. Norton & Company.

Lovink, G., Rossiter, N., & Ippolita, 2009. < nettime > The Digital Given – 10 Web 2.0 Theses by Ippolita, Geert Lovink, *Nettime Mailing List Archives*. Available at: http://www.nettime.org/Lists-Archives/nettime-l-0906/msg00028.html. [Accessed March 3, 2010.]

Mosca, G., 1960. *Ruling Class*, McGraw-Hill.

Parker, E., 2009. Is Technology Dumbing Down Japanese?, *New York Times*. Available at: http://www.nytimes.com/2009/11/08/books/review/EParker-t.html?_r=1&ref=books. [Accessed September 3, 2010.]

Richmond, R., 2009. Building an Online Bulwark to Fend Off Identity Fraud. *New York Times*. Available at: http://www.nytimes.com/2009/11/19/technology/personaltech/19basics.html. [Accessed September 3, 2010.]

Ries, B., 2010. Reddit Suicide: How the Internet Can Help and Hurt, *Daily Beast*. Available at: http://www.thedailybeast.com/blogs-and-stories/2010-08-31/reddit-suicide-how-the-internet-can-help-and-hurt/?cid=hp:beastoriginalsR3. [Accessed September 3, 2010.]

Rosen, J., 2009. Audience Atomization Overcome: Why the Internet Weakens the Authority of the Press, *PressThink*. Available at: http://journalism.nyu.edu/pubzone/weblogs/pressthink/2009/01/12/atomization.html. [Accessed September 9, 2010.]

Rossiter, N., 2008. Organized Networks, *Organized Networks: Invent New Institutional Forms*. Available at: http://nedrossiter.org/. [Accessed September 9, 2010.]

Steinhauer, J., 2008. Woman Indicted in MySpace Suicide Case, *New York Times*. Available at: http://www.nytimes.com/2008/05/16/us/16myspace.html. [Accessed September 3, 2010.]

Stone, B., 2009. Report Calls Online Threats to Children Overblown, *New York Times*. Available at: http://www.nytimes.com/2009/01/14/technology/internet/14cyberweb.html. [Accessed September 3, 2010.]

Wortham, J., 2010. Facebook Glitch Brings New Privacy Worries, *New York Times*. Available at: http://www.nytimes.com/2010/05/06/technology/internet/06facebook.html. [Accessed September 3, 2010.]

——, 2009. MySpace Turns Over 90,000 Names of Registered Sex Offenders, *New York Times*. Available at: http://www.nytimes.com/2009/02/04/technology/internet/04myspace.html. [Accessed September 3, 2010.]

WEBLOGRAPHY

Introduction

Twitter: http://www.twitter.com
Tumblr: http://www.tumblr.com
Google Image Search: http://www.google.com/imghp
Flickr: http://www.flickr.com

Chapter 1

Lawrence Lessig: http://www.lessig.org/blog/
Clay Shirky: http://www.shirky.com/
On Charles Babbage and the difference engine: http://www.computerhistory.
    org/babbage/
Telnet (ona1a): http://www.flickr.com/photos/ona1a/

Chapter 2

Jay Rosen: http://pressthink.org/
The Atlantic: http://www.theatlantic.com/
Talking Points Memo: http://www.talkingpointsmemo.com/
Wired Magazine: http://www.wired.com/ http://www.wired.com/culture/
    culturereviews/magazine/17-06/nep_newsocialism/
Kevin Kelly: http://www.kk.org/
Tech Crunch: http://techcrunch.com/

Chapter 3

danah boyd: http://www.danah.org/
MySpace: http://www.myspace.com/
Facebook: http://www.facebook.com/
Image of the Hudson River Plane Landing: http://twitpic.com/135xa
Clive Thompson: http://www.collisiondetection.net/
Daily Kos: http://www.dailykos.com/

Chapter 4

Tandy computer TV advertisement: http://www.youtube.com/watch?v=dl9kp2Pu6qs

Chapter 5

Edge: The Third Culture: http://www.edge.org/
Ned Rossiter: http://nedrossiter.org/

BIBLIOGRAPHY

2010. Britons "Multi-task" with Media, *BBC*. Available at: http://www.bbc.co.uk/news/technology-11012356. [Accessed August 21, 2010.]

2007. Facebook "Costs Businesses Dear," *BBC*. Available at: http://news.bbc.co.uk/2/hi/6989100.stm. [Accessed September 9, 2010.]

Facebook | Pages. Available at: http://www.facebook.com/advertising/?pages. [Accessed June 18, 2010.]

2010. multitasking, n. and adj. In *OED Online*. Available at: http://dictionary.oed.com.ezproxy.gc.cuny.edu/cgi/entry/00318370?query_type = word&queryword = multi-task&first = 1&max_to_show = 10&sort_type = alpha&result_place = 2. [Accessed August 21, 2010.]

Amazon, Amazon.com Help: Wireless, Whispernet, and Whispersync, *Amazon.com*. Available at: http://www.amazon.com/gp/help/customer/display.html?nodeId = 200375890. [Accessed August 27, 2010.]

Anderson, C. & Wolff, M., 2010. The Web is Dead. Long Live the Internet, *Wired*. Available at: http://www.wired.com/magazine/2010/08/ff_webrip/all/1. [Accessed August 22, 2010.]

Arnold, M., 1960. *Culture and Anarchy* (J. D. Wilson, ed.), Cambridge University Press

Arrington, M., 2008. Facebook No Longer The Second Largest Social Network, *TechCrunch*. Available at: http://techcrunch.com/2008/06/12/facebook-no-longer-the-second-largest-social-network/. [Accessed July 21, 2010.]

Arrington, M., 2008. Facebook Responds To MySpace With Facebook Connect, *TechCrunch*. Available at: http://techcrunch.com/2008/05/09/facebook-responds-to-myspace-with-facebook-connect/. [Accessed July 22, 2010.]

Arrington, M., 2007. 2 Billion Photos On Flickr, *TechCrunch*. Available at: http://techcrunch.com/2007/11/13/2-billion-photos-on-flickr/. [Accessed May 29, 2010.]

Barthes, R. & Heath, S., 1978. The Death of the Author. In *Image, Music, Text*, Macmillan.

BBC News, 2005. Microsoft Aims to Trounce Google, *BBC*. Available at: http://news.bbc.co.uk/2/hi/technology/4382112.stm. [Accessed July 25, 2010.]

Benjamin, W. & Arendt, H., 1969. The Work of Art in the Age of Mechanical Reproduction. In *Illuminations*, Schocken Books.

Bilton, N., 2010. Bits Pics: Twitter Traffic During the World Cup, *Bits Blog*. Available at: http://bits.blogs.nytimes.com/2010/07/17/bits-pics-twitter-usage-during-the-world-cup/. [Accessed August 21, 2010.]

Bilton, N., 2010. No E-Books Allowed in This Establishment, *Bits Blog*. Available at: http://bits.blogs.nytimes.com/2010/08/02/no-e-books-allowed-in-this-establishment/. [Accessed August 21, 2010.]

Bolter, J.D. & Grusin, R., 2000. *Remediation: Understanding New Media*, MIT Press.

Bourdieu, P., 1993. *The Field of Cultural Production*, Columbia University Press.

boyd, d. & Ellison, N., 2007. Social Network Sites: Definition, History, and Scholarship, *Journal of Computer-Mediated Communication*, 13(1). Available at: http://jcmc.indiana.edu/vol13/issue1/boyd.ellison.html. [Accessed July 17, 2010.]

Buckley, C. & Richtel, M., 2010. Good Cellphone Service Comes at a Price. *New York Times*. Available at: http://www.nytimes.com/2010/08/21/nyregion/21celltower.html?_r = 1&hp. [Accessed August 20, 2010.]

Carlson, B., 2009. About Us | The Atlantic Wire, *The Atlantic*. Available at: http://www.theatlanticwire.com/opinions/view/opinion/About-Us-1003. [Accessed May 25, 2010.]

Carr, D., 2010. Why Twitter Will Endure. *New York Times*. Available at: http://www.nytimes.com/2010/01/03/weekinreview/03carr.html. [Accessed September 9, 2010.]

Carr, N., 2010. *The Shallows: How the Internet is Changing the Way We Think, Read and Remember*, Atlantic Books.

Carr, N., 2010. The Web Shatters Focus, Rewires Brains, *Wired*, 18(09). Available at: http://www.wired.com/magazine/2010/05/ff_nicholas_carr/all/1. [Accessed September 5, 2010.]

Carr, N., 2008. Is Google Making Us Stupid?, *The Atlantic*, July/August. Available at: http://www.theatlantic.com/magazine/archive/2008/07/is-google-making-us-stupid/6868/. [Accessed September 3, 2010.]

Castells, M., 2000. Toward a Sociology of the Network Society, *Contemporary Sociology*, 29(5), 693–99.

Cellan-Jones, R., 2010. E-books: Amazon Bites Back, *dot. Rory: A blog about technology*. Available at: http://www.bbc.co.uk/blogs/thereporters/rorycellan-jones/2010/07/ebooks_amazon_bites_back.html. [Accessed August 27, 2010.]

Cellan-Jones, R., 2010. A Multi-tasking Moral Panic, *dot. Rory: A blog about technology*. Available at: http://www.bbc.co.uk/blogs/thereporters/rorycellanjones/2010/08/a_multi-tasking_moral_panic.html. [Accessed August 21, 2010.]

Cellan-Jones, R., 2009. Twitter and a Classic Picture, *dot.life*. Available at: http://www.bbc.co.uk/blogs/technology/2009/01/twitter_and_a_classic_picture.html. [Accessed July 24, 2010.]

Chapman, C., 2009. The History of the Internet in a Nutshell, *Six Revisions*. Available at: http://sixrevisions.com/resources/the-history-of-the-internet-in-a-nutshell/. [Accessed May 17, 2010.]

Clough, P.T., 1994. *Feminist Thought: Desire, Power, and Academic Discourse*, Blackwell.

Coleman, E.G. & Golub, A., 2008. Hacker Practice: Moral Genres and the Cultural Articulation of Liberalism, *Anthropological Theory*, 8(3), 255–77.

Coleman, G., 2009. Code is Speech: Legal Tinkering, Expertise, and Protest among Free and Open Source Software Developers, *Cultural Anthropology*, 24(3), 420–54.

Connelly, P., 2009. The Life and Death of Online Communities | The American Prospect, *The American Prospect*. Available at: http://www.prospect.org/cs/articles?article = neo_cities. [Accessed July 26, 2010.]

Craig, T. & Shear, M., 2006. Allen Quip Provokes Outrage, Apology, *Washington Post*. Available at: http://www.washingtonpost.com/wp-dyn/content/article/2006/08/14/AR2006081400589.html. [Accessed September 8, 2010.]

Daily Kos, Daily Kos: About Daily Kos. Available at: http://www.dailykos.com/special/about2#dk. [Accessed July 15, 2010.]

Davis, L., 2009. Facebook Plans to Make Money by Selling Your Data, *Read Write Web*. Available at: http://www.readwriteweb.com/archives/facebook_sells_your_data.php. [Accessed June 7, 2010.]

De Landa, M., 1991. *War in the Age of Intelligent Machines*, Zone Books.

Deleuze, G. & Guattari, F., 1987. *A Thousand Plateaus: Capitalism and Schizophrenia*, University of Minnesota Press.

Dibbell, J., 2005. Pic Your Friends, *The Village Voice*. Available at: http://www.villagevoice.com/2005-03-22/screens/pic-your-friends/. [Accessed May 28, 2010.]

Economist, 2009. The Internet at Forty, *The Economist*. Available at: http://www.economist.com/sciencetechnology/displaystory.cfm?story_id = 14391822. [Accessed April 14, 2010.]

Elliott, A. & Urry, J., 2010. *Mobile Lives*, Routledge.

Ellul, J., 1964. *The Technological Society*, Vintage Books.

Featherstone, M., 2009. Ubiquitous Media: An Introduction, *Theory, Culture & Society*, 26(2–3), 1.

Feenberg, A., 1991. *Critical Theory of Technology*, Oxford University Press.

Foucault, M., 1984. What is an Author? In *The Foucault Reader*, Vintage.

Friedberg, A., 2006. *The Virtual Window: From Alberti to Microsoft*, MIT Press.

Friedman, T.L., 2005, *The World Is Flat: A Brief History of the Twenty-first Century*, Farrar, Straus & Giroux.

Galloway, A., 2007. 24/7, 16.8: Is 24 a Political Show?, *Afterimage*, 35(1), 18–22.

Galloway, A.R., 2004. *Protocol*, MIT Press.

Gasset, J.O.Y., 1994. *The Revolt of the Masses*, W. W. Norton & Company.

Goodman, J.D., 2010. Drinking Game Poses Query, Who's "Icing" Whom?, *New York Times*. Available at: http://www.nytimes.com/2010/06/09/business/media/09adco.html?_r = 1&ref = media. [Accessed August 28, 2010.]

Granovetter, M.S., 1973. The Strength of Weak Ties, *American Journal of Sociology*, 78(6), 1360–80.

Grossman, L., 2006. Time's Person of the Year: You, *Time*. Available at: http://www.time.com/time/magazine/article/0,9171,1569514,00.html. [Accessed March 3, 2010.]

Han, S., 2007. *Navigating Technomedia: Caught in the Web*, Rowman & Littlefield.

Haraway, D., 1992. The Promises of Monsters, *Cultural Studies*, 295–337.

Haraway, D.J., 1990. *Simians, Cyborgs, and Women: The Reinvention of Nature*, Routledge.

Hardt, M., 1999. Affective Labor, *Boundary 2*, 89–100.

Hardt, M. & Negri, A., 2001. *Empire*, Harvard University Press.

Helft, M. & Vega, T., 2010. Retargeting Ads Follow Surfers to Other Sites, *New York Times*. Available at: http://www.nytimes.com/2010/08/30/technology/30adstalk.html?_r = 1. [Accessed September 9, 2010.]

Howard, T., 2004. "Can You Hear Me Now?" A Hit, *USA Today*. Available at: http://www.usatoday.com/money/advertising/adtrack/2004-02-22-track-verizon_x.htm. [Accessed August 20, 2010.]

Howe, J., 2008. *Crowdsourcing: Why the Power of the Crowd Is Driving the Future of Business*, Crown Business.

Jenkins, H., 2006. *Convergence Culture: Where Old and New Media Collide*, New York University Press.

Jenkins, H., 1992. *Textual Poachers: Television Fans and Participatory Culture*, Routledge.

Jenkins, H., Li, X., Domb Krauskopf, A., & Green, J., 2009. If It Doesn't Spread, It's Dead (Parts 1–8), *MIT Convergence Culture Consortium*. Available at: http://www.convergenceculture.org/weblog/2009/02/if_it_doesnt_spread_its_dead_p_7.php#more. [Accessed August 26, 2010.]

Keen, A., 2007. *The Cult of the Amateur: How Today's Internet is Killing Our Culture*, Crown Business.

Kelly, K., 2009. The New Socialism: Global Collectivist Society Is Coming Online, *Wired*, 17(06). Available at: http://www.wired.com/culture/culturereviews/magazine/17-06/nep_newsocialism. [Accessed June 5, 2010.]

Kim, E. & Gilbert, S., 2009. *Detecting Sadness in 140 Characters*. Available at: http://www.webecologyproject.org/2009/08/detecting-sadness-in-140-characters/. [Accessed July 24, 2010.]

Kittler, F., 2005. There is No Software, *CTheory.net*. Available at: http://www.ctheory.net/articles.aspx?id = 74. [Accessed March 4, 2010.]

Kittler, F., 1996. The History of Communication Media, *CTheory*, (ga114). Available at: http://www.ctheory.net/articles.aspx?id = 45. [Accessed July 16, 2010.]

Krums, J., 2009. Twitter / Janis Krums: http://twitpic.com/135xa – . . ., *Twitter*. Available at: http://twitter.com/jkrums/status/1121915133. [Accessed July 24, 2010.]

Lanier, J., 2010. The End of Human Specialness, *The Chronicle of Higher Education*. Available at: http://chronicle.com/article/article-content/124124/. [Accessed September 4, 2010.]

Lanier, J., 2010. *You Are Not a Gadget: A Manifesto*, Knopf.

Lanier, J., 2006. DIGITAL MAOISM: The Hazards of the New Online Collectivism, *Edge: The Third Culture*. Available at: http://www.edge.org/3rd_culture/lanier06/lanier06_index.html. [Accessed September 4, 2010.]

Lasch, C., 1991. *The Culture of Narcissism: American Life in an Age of Diminishing Expectations* rev. edn, W. W. Norton & Company.

Lash, S., 2002. *Critique of Information*, Sage.

Lehrer, B., 2010. Inspector Gadget: Over-Deviced (March 04, 2010), *The Brian Lehrer Show*. Available at: http://www.wnyc.org/shows/bl/episodes/2010/03/04/segments/151129. [Accessed March 4, 2010.]

Leiner, B. et al., 2003. A Brief HIstory of the Internet, *Internet Society*. Available at: http://www.isoc.org/internet/history/brief.shtml. [Accessed April 15, 2010.]

Lessig, L., 2009. On "Socialism": Round II (Lessig Blog), *Lessig*. Available at: http://www.lessig.org/blog/2009/05/on_socialism_round_ii.html. [Accessed June 8, 2010.]

Lessig, L., 2008. *Remix: Making Art and Commerce Thrive in the Hybrid Economy*, Penguin.

Lessig, L., 2001. *The Future of Ideas*, Random House.

Levy, P., 2001. *Cyberculture*, University of Minnesota Press.

Levy, P., 1997. *Collective Intelligence*, Basic Books.

Lewine, I.B.E., 2007. The Encyclopedist's Lair, *New York Times Magazine*. Available at: http://www.nytimes.com/2007/11/18/magazine/18wwln-domains-t.html. [Accessed May 18, 2010.]

Lohr, S., 2010. Now Playing: Night of the Living Tech, *New York Times*. Available at: http://www.nytimes.com/2010/08/22/weekinreview/22lohr.html?_r = 1. [Accessed August 22, 2010.]

Lovink, G., 2007. *Zero Comments: Blogging and Critical Internet Culture*, Routledge.

Lovink, G., Rossiter, N., & Ippolita, 2009. < nettime > The Digital Given – 10 Web 2.0 Theses by Ippolita, Geert Lovink, *Nettime Mailing List Archives*. Available at: http://www.nettime.org/Lists-Archives/nettime-l-0906/msg00028.html. [Accessed March 3, 2010.]

Mackenzie, A., 2005. Untangling the Unwired: Wi-Fi and the Cultural Inversion of Infrastructure, *Space and Culture*, 8(3), 269.

Maffesoli, M., 1993. The Social Ambiance, *Current Sociology*, 41(2), 1–15.

Manovich, L., 2007. *The Language of New Media*, MIT Press.

Massing, M., 2009. The News About the Internet, *New York Review of Books*, (13 August 2009). Available at: http://www.nybooks.com/articles/archives/2009/aug/13/the-news-about-the-internet/. [Accessed June 1, 2010.]

McClellan, J., 2005. Tag Team, *Guardian*. Available at: http://www.guardian.co.uk/technology/2005/feb/03/onlinesupplement? [Accessed May 20, 2010.]

McLuhan, M., 1969. Marshall McLuhan—A Candid Conversation with the High Priest of Popcult and Metaphysician of Media, *Playboy*, March, 233–69.

McLuhan, M., 1964. *Understanding Media: The Extensions of Man*, Signet.

Miller, C.C., 2010. Starbucks to Offer Free Wi-Fi, *New York Times*. Available at: http://www.nytimes.com/2010/06/15/technology/15starbux.html?scp = 1&sq = starbucks%20wifi&st = cse. [Accessed August 27, 2010.]

Moore, T., 2003. Camp Aims to Beat Web Addiction, *BBC.* Available at: http://news.bbc.co.uk/2/hi/europe/3125475.stm. [Accessed July 15, 2010.]

Mosca, G., 1960. *Ruling Class,* McGraw-Hill.

Myers, R., 2010. The GNU Operating System, *GNU Operating System.* Available at: http://www.gnu.org/. [Accessed May 17, 2010.]

Neate, R. & Mason, R., 2009. Networking Site Cashes in On Friends, *Telegraph. co.uk.* Available at: http://www.telegraph.co.uk/finance/newsbysector/mediatechnologyandtelecoms/4413483/Networking-site-cashes-in-on-friends.html. [Accessed June 7, 2010.]

O'Reilly, T., 2005. What is Web 2.0: Design Patterns and Business Models for the Next Generation of Software, *O'Reilly Media.* Available at: http://oreilly.com/web2/archive/what-is-web-20.html. [Accessed May 21, 2010.]

O'Reilly, T. & Battelle, J., 2009. Web Squared: Web 2.0 Five Years On, *Web 2.0 Summit.* Available at: http://www.web2summit.com/web2009/public/schedule/detail/10194. [Accessed March 3, 2010.]

Odlyzko, A., 2001. Content is Not King, *First Monday*, 6(2). Available at: http://firstmonday.org/htbin/cgiwrap/bin/ojs/index.php/fm/article/viewArticle/833/742. [Accessed June 2, 2010.]

Oliver, S.S., 2010. Who Elected Me Mayor on Foursquare? I Did, *New York Times.* Available at: http://www.nytimes.com/2010/08/19/fashion/19foursquare.html?ref = technology. [Accessed August 27, 2010.]

Ong, W.J., 2002. *Orality and Literacy: The Technologizing of the Word,* Routledge.

Ong, W.J., 1967. *The Presence of the Word: Some Prolegomena for Cultural and Religious History,* Yale University Press.

Parker, E., 2009. Is Technology Dumbing Down Japanese?, *New York Times.* Available at: http://www.nytimes.com/2009/11/08/books/review/EParker-t.html?_r = 1&ref = books. [Accessed September 3, 2010.]

PC Magazine, API. In *PCMag.com Encyclopedia.* Available at: http://www.pcmag.com/encyclopedia_term/0,2542,t = API&i = 37856,00.asp. [Accessed July 22, 2010.]

Pink, D.H., 2005. Folksonomy, *New York Times.* Available at: http://www.nytimes.com/2005/12/11/magazine/11ideas1–21.html?_r = 1. [Accessed May 28, 2010.]

Raymond, E.S., 2002. *The Cathedral and the Bazaar.* Available at: http://www.catb.org/ esr/writings/cathedral-bazaar/cathedral-bazaar/. [Accessed May 19, 2010.]

Rheingold, H., 2000. *The Virtual Community: Homesteading on the Electronic Frontier* rev. edn, MIT Press.

Richmond, R., 2009. Building an Online Bulwark to Fend Off Identity Fraud, *New York Times.* Available at: http://www.nytimes.com/2009/11/19/technology/personaltech/19basics.html. [Accessed September 3, 2010.]

Ries, B., 2010. Reddit Suicide: How the Internet Can Help and Hurt, *Daily Beast.* Available at: http://www.thedailybeast.com/blogs-and-stories/2010-08-31/reddit-suicide-how-the-internet-can-help-and-hurt/?cid = hp:beastoriginalsR3. [Accessed September 3, 2010.]

Rose, J., 2005. *Sexuality in the Field of Vision,* Verso.

Rosen, J., 2009. Audience Atomization Overcome: Why the Internet Weakens the Authority of the Press, *PressThink.* Available at: http://journalism.nyu.

edu/pubzone/weblogs/pressthink/2009/01/12/atomization.html. [Accessed September 9, 2010.]

Rosen, J., 2006. Web Users Open the Gates, *Washington Post*. Available at: http://www.washingtonpost.com/wp-dyn/content/article/2006/06/18/AR2006061800618.html. [Accessed May 25, 2010.]

Rossiter, N., 2008. Organized Networks, *Organized Networks: Invent New Institutional Forms*. Available at: http://nedrossiter.org/. [Accessed September 9, 2010.]

Saborio, W., 2010. Breaking the Ice – "Shirley Tilghman: Not a Bro", *The Ink*. Available at: http://www.universitypressclub.com/archive/2010/06/one-ice-later-shirley-tilghman-not-a-bro/. [Accessed August 28, 2010.]

Sanders, J., Nee, V., & Sernau, S., 2002. Asian Immigrants' Reliance on Social Ties in a Multiethnic Labor Market, *Social Forces*, 81, 281.

Sanghvi, R., 2006. Facebook Gets a Facelift | Facebook, *Facebook Blog*. Available at: http://blog.facebook.com/blog.php?post = 2207967130. [Accessed July 23, 2010.]

Scanella, C., 2008. *Mundane Blogging: The Medium and Social Practices of Daily Kos*, New School.

Scheler, M.F., 1983. *Nature of Sympathy*, Shoe String Press.

Schonfeld, E., 2010. Costolo: Twitter Now Has 190 Million Users Tweeting 65 Million Times A Day, *TechCrunch*. Available at: http://techcrunch.com/2010/06/08/twitter-190-million-users/. [Accessed July 21, 2010.]

Schonfeld, E., 2009. Facebook's Response To Twitter, *TechCrunch*. Available at: http://techcrunch.com/2009/03/04/facebooks-response-to-twitter/. [Accessed July 23, 2010.]

Sheller, M. & Urry, J., 2006. The New Mobilities Paradigm, *Environment and Planning A*, 38(2), 207.

Shiels, M., 2010. iPad to "Kickstart" Tablet Market, *BBC*. Available at: http://news.bbc.co.uk/2/hi/technology/8484395.stm. [Accessed August 21, 2010.]

Shirky, C., 2003. Social Software and the Politics of Groups, *Clay Shirky's Writings About the Internet*. Available at: http://www.shirky.com/writings/group_politics.html. [Accessed June 5, 2010.]

Shirky, C., 1999. The Open Source Interest Horizon, *Clay Shirky's Writings About the Internet*. Available at: http://www.shirky.com/writings/interest.html. [Accessed May 20, 2010.]

Shirky, C., 1996. In Praise of Evolvable Systems, *Clay Shirky's Writings About the Internet*. Available at: http://www.shirky.com/writings/evolve.html. [Accessed May 19, 2010.]

Siegler, M., 2010. Just In Time For The Location Wars, Twitter Turns On Geolocation On Its Website, *TechCrunch*. Available at: http://techcrunch.com/2010/03/09/twitter-location-website/. [Accessed August 27, 2010.]

Sillito, D., 2009. Twitter's Iconic Image of US Airways Plane, *BBC News*. Available at: http://news.bbc.co.uk/2/hi/americas/7834755.stm. [Accessed July 24, 2010.]

Slim, F., 2010. Guest Op Ed: Why Bros Get Iced, Bro, *The Awl*. Available at: http://www.theawl.com/2010/05/guest-op-ed-why-bros-get-iced-bro. [Accessed August 28, 2010.]

Stallman, R., 2000. Re: Evaluation of Gcompris. Available at: http://www.gnu. org/encyclopedia/anencyc.txt. [Accessed May 17, 2010.]

Steinhauer, J., 2008. Woman Indicted in MySpace Suicide Case, *New York Times*. Available at: http://www.nytimes.com/2008/05/16/us/16myspace. html. [Accessed September 3, 2010.]

Stiegler, B., 2009. Teleologics of the Snail: The Errant Self Wired to a WiMax Network, *Theory, Culture & Society*, 26(2–3), 33.

Stone, B., 2009. Report Calls Online Threats to Children Overblown, *New York Times*. Available at: http://www.nytimes.com/2009/01/14/technology/internet/ 14cyberweb.html. [Accessed September 3, 2010.]

Stone, B., 2008. Control Lights with Twitter, *Twitter Blog*. Available at: http://blog. twitter.com/2008/05/control-lights-with-twitter.html. [Accessed July 22, 2010.]

Stone, B. & Williams, E., 2010. *Is Twitter a Force for Good?* Available at: http://www. bbc.co.uk/news/technology-10652690. [Accessed July 19, 2010.]

Strand, O., 2010. The New Coffee Bars: Unplug, Drink Up, *New York Times*. Available at: http://www.nytimes.com/2010/08/25/dining/25coffee.html?_ r = 2&src = tptw. [Accessed August 28, 2010.]

Thompson, C., 2009. Clive Thompson on How the Real-Time Web Is Leaving Google Behind, *Wired*, 17(10). Available at: http://www.wired.com/techbiz/ people/magazine/17–10/st_thompson. [Accessed July 24, 2010.]

Thompson, C., 2007. Clive Thompson on How Twitter Creates a Social Sixth Sense, *Wired*, 15(07). Available at: http://www.wired.com/techbiz/media/ magazine/15–07/st_thompson. [Accessed July 13, 2010.]

Tiessen, M., 2007. Urban Meanderthals and the City of "Desire Lines", *CTheory.net*. Available at: http://www.ctheory.net/articles.aspx?id = 583. [Accessed August 28, 2010.]

Torrone, P., 2004. Interview with Caterina Fake from Flickr, *Engadget*. Available at: http://www.engadget.com/2004/12/03/interview-with-caterina-fake-from-flickr/. [Accessed May 29, 2010.]

Turkle, S., 2005. *The Second Self*, MIT Press.

Turkle, S., 1997. *Life on the Screen: Identity in the Age of the Internet*, Simon & Schuster.

Vance, A. & Richtel, M., 2009. Light and Cheap, Netbooks Are Poised to Reshape PC Industry, *New York Times*. Available at: http://www.nytimes.com/2009/04/02/ technology/02netbooks.html?_r = 1&scp = 3&sq = netbook&st = Search. [Accessed August 21, 2010.]

Vander Wal, T., 2007. Folksonomy: vanderwal.net, *Vanderwal.net*. Available at: http://www.vanderwal.net/folksonomy.html. [Accessed May 30, 2010.]

Wald, M.L., 2009. Plane Crew Is Credited for Nimble Reaction, *New York Times*. Available at: http://www.nytimes.com/2009/01/16/nyregion/16pilot.html. [Accessed July 24, 2010.]

Warren, C., 2009. New Flip Video Camera Includes Direct Facebook Uploads, *Mashable*. Available at: http://mashable.com/2009/10/14/new-flip-video-camera-includes-direct-facebook-uploads/. [Accessed August 28, 2010.]

Wickett, J., 2010. Control Lights with Twitter, *Vimeo*. Available at: http://vimeo. com/1025711. [Accessed July 22, 2010.]

Wiener, N., 1965. *Cybernetics or Control and Communication in the Animal and the Machine*, MIT Press.

Wortham, J., 2010. Facebook Glitch Brings New Privacy Worries, *New York Times*. Available at: http://www.nytimes.com/2010/05/06/technology/internet/06facebook.html. [Accessed September 3, 2010.]

Wortham, J., 2009. Face-to-Face Socializing Starts With a Mobile Post, *New York Times*. Available at: http://www.nytimes.com/2009/10/19/technology/internet/19foursquare.html?ref = technology. [Accessed August 27, 2010.]

Wortham, J., 2009. MySpace Turns Over 90,000 Names of Registered Sex Offenders, *New York Times*. Available at: http://www.nytimes.com/2009/02/04/technology/internet/04myspace.html. [Accessed September 3, 2010.]

INDEX